D0021729

The Spirit *of* Disobedience

Also by Curtis White
The Middle Mind: Why Americans Don't Think for Themselves
Monstrous Possibility: An Invitation to Literary Politics
Requiem
Memories of My Father Watching TV
America's Magic Mountain
The Idea of Home
Anarcho Hindu
Metaphysics in the Midwest
Heretical Songs

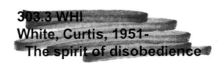
CURTIS WHITE

The Spirit *of* Disobedience

Resisting the Charms of Fake Politics,
Mindless Consumption,
and the Culture of Total Work

PoliPointPress

The Spirit of Disobedience: Resisting the Charms of Fake Politics, Mindless Consumption, and the Culture of Total Work
by Curtis White

This edition published in the United States of America by
PoliPointPress, P.O. Box 3008, Sausalito, CA 94966-3008.
www.p3books.com

Production management: Michael Bass Associates
Book design: Michael Bass Associates
Cover design: Jeff Kenyon

Library of Congress Cataloging-in-Publication Data
White, Curtis, 1951–
    The spirit of disobedience: resisting the charms of fake politics, mindless
consumption, and the culture of total work / Curtis White.
      p.   cm.
    ISBN-13: 978-0-9778253-1-8
    1. Social values—United States. 2. Political culture—United States. 3. Right
and left (Political science) 4. Spirituality—Social aspects. I. Title.
    HN65.W488 2007
    303.3'720973—dc22

                                                                    2006026272

Printed in the United States of America
October 2006

Published by:
PoliPointPress, LLC
P.O. Box 3008
Sausalito, CA 94966-3008
(415) 339-4100
www.p3books.com

Distributed by Publishers Group West

For Gilbert Sorrentino, disobedient spirit,
1929–2006

Contents

Introduction   1

Chapter 1   Imagination Dead Imagine   19

Chapter 2   Beyond the Golden Rule   45

Chapter 3   Confessions of a Holy Whore   69

Chapter 4   The Spirit of Disobedience   95

Chapter 5   A New Fundamentalism:
Time, Home, and Food   121

Epilogue   161
Notes   163
Bibliography   169
Acknowledgments   173
Index   175
About the Author   183

Introduction

1.

I would like to introduce two ideas that are essential to what I am calling the spirit of disobedience. These two ideas are simple enough to state but more complicated to demonstrate. They both involve old delusions of American liberalism. The first delusion is that liberal/left politics, in both theory and action, is somehow independent of a need for the spiritual. To the contrary, I think I can show that it has always, whether it has known it or not, been dependent on assumptions that are finally spiritual, and this goes for notoriously antireligious thinkers like Karl Marx and Immanuel Kant as well. The second point is related but runs in the opposite direction. That thing—Reason—that liberalism has always assumed to be a secular force, the gift of its Enlightenment heroes of science and philosophy, is also finally spiritual but in the worst possible sense, it is *religious*. Reason is that thing that liberalism has itself always claimed to despise: a baseless and destructive enthusiasm.

We have seen a renaissance in a "faith in Reason" in recent years, especially since liberalism's humiliating defeat at the hands of evangelical America in the 2004 national elections. Following that election, there was an immediate roar from the disappointed. In an op-ed piece, historian Garry Wills suggested that the Republican/evangelical triumph was in fact the end of critical intelligence, the unhappy victory of religious superstition, intolerance, cruelty, torture, and so forth. The Bush victory was, in short, the death of the Enlightenment.[1] According to Wills, four hundred years of progress had been dashed by a bunch of fundamentalist evangelicals in rural Ohio, and we were going to have to start all over again. Summon old Voltaire from his cranky grave. Storm the Bastille. Why, Sisyphus had it easy in comparison.

Then, cruelest blow of all, the web lit up with a chart cobbled together by one Christopher Evans from his personal web site where, among other things, he studies the musculature of the shoulder carriage. His infamous post to the web purported to show that the average IQ of "red" Republican states was far below the average IQ of "blue" Democratic states. It was as if American liberals were saying, "The Republicans may have won, but they should be *embarrassed* about it." It had been reasonably shown (Evans used statistics!) that evangelical Republicans were stupid.

Bill Maher, appearing on MSNBC's *Scarborough Country* in support of the Wills column, summed up the self-satisfied perspective of liberal America in saying, "I am just embarrassed that [America] has been taken over by people like evangelicals, by people who do not believe in science and rationality."[2]

But the smugness of a purportedly secular liberalism, confidently established in the powers of Reason, does not bear up well under examination. Is it really so free of the religious prejudice and superstition it has always claimed to despise? Has it no need for the spiritual?

2.

Karl Marx famously assumed that his criticism of capitalism was independent of any religious thought and that, in fact, it implied the destruction of religion as such. Good, reasonable son of the Enlightenment that he was, he could describe how capitalism functioned, as a sort of exploitation machine, which is exactly what he did through the concept of "surplus value" developed endlessly in *Capital* (1867). In essence, surplus value is a way of accounting for the difference between the value a laborer creates through work and the value he receives back as wages. The difference, or surplus, is what the capitalist keeps to pay for the expense of doing business and as profit, whether in his own pocket or in the pocket of his shareholders in the age of the corporation. As this surplus accumulates it becomes *capital* and seals the fate of the working class, always now dependent on the interests and ambitions of the owners of what Marx called the "means of production." Henceforth, private abundance will assure public destitution. Even more ominously, the worker is now dependent on the capitalist's sense of justice. To the worker the capitalist says, "This is what will count as fair in this social order." As Jean-Jacques Rousseau put it in *The Social Contract* (1762), speaking of the absurdity of a "right" to slavery, "I make with you a convention wholly at your expense and wholly to my advantage; I shall keep it as long as I like, and you will keep it as long as I like." For Marx, the social agreement made by capitalism with its "wage slaves" was no less absurd and one-sided. But for the capitalist, the only meaningful question of justice is the pragmatic question: How far can these "slaves" be made the sacrificial victims of our well-being before they revolt? How can we convince them to accept their role as economic scapegoats in this system?

More important, Marx could describe how capitalism was *experienced* by human beings, which he did through the concept of "alienation" in his early essays, like "The Economic and Philosophic Manuscripts of 1844" (written just a year before Henry David Thoreau would begin his famous retreat from his own sense of economic alienation to Walden Pond). Because the logic of capitalism tends toward ever more radical models of efficiency in order to maximize the creation of surplus value, and because it is more efficient to consider the human beings standing before it only as the purely contractual offer of their labor capacity, all other human attributes—the spiritual, certainly, but also the creative—become somebody else's problem. This is the logic that, to this day, even parents and school boards apply when they decide that music education (or art or the girls' tennis team) is a luxury and that the only essentials in the curriculum are those that will lead most directly to employability. As state legislators are wont to say in that poetic way of theirs: the only justification for education is "workforce preparation." More brutally put (as if that bureaucratic phrasing weren't brutal enough), through education the protectors of children prepare their young charges for future roles as labor commodities.

Strangely, Marx could never say why any of this was wrong. He could claim that this thing called a "human" had a "concept" (what Marx awkwardly called "species being") and that capitalism denied this thing's essence, as if a wildebeest were instructed to live like an ibis. But in the end this is mere metaphysical question begging. Marx assumed what he needed to show: that capitalism does what it oughtn't, that, in short, it is immoral. What Marx most conspicuously lacked was an ethic, a motive for his own critical work, and what he needed but most resisted was Spirit.

For Marx, religion represented the self-destructive superstitions of people who did not understand the true meaning of their own real conditions. But without some spiritual underpinning, Marx's analysis is always vulnerable to the simplest sort of objection: "So what?" Capitalism exploits, you say. So what? Why shouldn't it? You don't even know what you mean by "exploitation," argues the capitalist. This thing you call exploitation is merely an agreement, freely entered into, in which the worker willingly exchanges her capacity to work for wages. And that agreement is just part of a larger social contract that allows for inequalities in wealth in the name of the common good. That is in the end what you mean by "inequality": the acceptance of differences in wealth that in reality provide for the wealth of the community as a whole. By eliminating these differences, you threaten everyone's well-being. So, since you can't say what you mean by "exploitation," it's a moot point and certainly no cause for this even more dubious thing you call a revolution.

Or, you say, capitalism dehumanizes or alienates. So what? Who said it shouldn't? What's "human," anyway? How do you

4

know anything about essential human qualities? (Even our post-modern professors, politically leftist though they try to be, would have to object, "Why, that's essentializing! We leave talking about the 'inestimable value of human life' to the pope.") And the truth is that Marx didn't know anything more about these essential ethical and spiritual questions than the capitalist, and neither did the "science" he inspired, Marxism. Marx's *Capital* as a description of a political economy is ethically neutral *in theory*. Marxism may assume kinds of grievance and kinds of damage, and Marx himself may generate indignation over the treatment of workers with a satirical brio worthy of Jonathan Swift, but neither Marx nor Marxism has ever demonstrated the ethical basis for its objections to life under capital. He couldn't, and it can't. So Marx didn't waste his time with a philosophical ethics; he just assumed the ethical basis he needed for his critique of capitalism. But what did he assume and where did it come from?

Marx's reluctance to enter the philosophical battle over ethics is perhaps because he saw it for what it had been: an endless intellectual quagmire. Had he been required to provide an assured ethic, he would never have gotten to what he truly wished to do, describe, criticize, and destroy capitalism. His purpose was, famously, to *change* the world. As he certainly understood, the history of the metaphysics of ethics was in fact a long and dubious intellectual project, and it was perhaps simply a spectacular failure.

The most notable of these failures was Kant's *Critique of Practical Reason* (1788) and *Foundations of the Metaphysics of Morals* (1785). Kant's *Critique* was the most ambitious response of the Enlightenment to the anxious suspicion that it had itself killed morality in the process of debunking Christianity (a debunking for which Kant was popularly considered largely responsible; in his time he was referred to as the "all-crushing," the destroyer of religion). And in fact Kant did make a certain kind of Christian ethic very difficult to maintain. For example, the Christian ethicist William Paley proposed, in his *Principles of Moral and Political Philosophy* (1785), that being ethical meant simply being consistent with the will of God, and God's

5

will was known through scripture. For orthodox Christians, this position has lost none of its power to persuade in the last 250 years. But after Diderot, Voltaire, and Kant, no thinking person could hope to assert the authority of the Bible without bringing scorn upon himself. That the Bible was a document not of divine guidance but of *prejudice* was, for sophisticated people, a settled matter.

The problem that developed for secularists was in knowing how to critique the ethics of religious revelation without simply creating a void. Our own Thomas Paine worried, in chapter 1 of *The Age of Reason* (1794), that "a work of this kind [is] exceedingly necessary, lest, in the general wreck of superstition, of false systems of government, and false theology, we lose sight of morality, of humanity, and of the theology that is true." So Paine, like Kant and many others, worked philosophically to fill the lack created by the Enlightenment critique of religion. Kant proposed the idea that something called Reason, properly understood, could function as an ethical "faculty."[3]

This was a revolutionary idea and, as Kant developed it, an idea of genius, but it was not without its own problems. As is usually the case with the creators of revolutionary thought, Kant's subtleties—especially the ways in which his philosophy *limits* the authority of Reason—were lost on many of his advocates, often with bloody consequences. In the heady aftermath of the Enlightenment, many European radicals felt confident enough in the viability of Kant's achievement to, essentially, establish a secular religion of Reason. For instance (and a gaudy instance it is), the leaders of the Paris Commune in 1793 actually went so far as to hold ceremonies to the Goddess of Reason in the Cathedral of Notre Dame! Stranger yet, among these celebrants were the architects of the Terror, people like Robespierre, a man who, in Andre Maurois's phrase, "knew himself to be so incorruptible that he denied himself no crime." Thus the ethics of Reason in its first full flight of confidence: the guillotine. (And we thought Ockham's razor was sharp!) But even as late as the Third Republic in the 1880s, liberal politicians like Jules Ferry were attempting to deprive the Catholic Church of the right to teach and instituting a secular morality in the "godless school" through which middle-class boys were taught—guess what?—the metaphysics of Kant!

The confidence of Monsieur Ferry has really never left liberalism as the editorial page of your local newspaper probably demonstrates. Here in Bloomington-Normal, Illinois, the biblical moralists trade blows with advocates of secular morality on an almost daily basis in the editorial pages of the *Pantagraph*. For instance, on January 14, 2005, a letter to the editor claimed that God was a virus that has "infected the mind of man" and that it is "preposterous" to think that "religion has a monopoly on morality." But then, ah!, the clouds part, "it is through the exercise of reason, sound judgment and the acquisition of general knowledge . . . that we know right from wrong."

In spite of the frightening confidence with which this secular morality is forwarded, it should be clear that the descendants of the Enlightenment have replaced the ethics of Christian revelation with something not a lot less mysterious. Just what is this capacity called Reason? In his famous essay "What Is Enlightenment?" Kant argues that enlightenment is the free use of one's reason. But he does not ask, "What is reason?" (anymore than he asks whether there is really something called "morality"). Reason becomes for Kant what he himself calls a "prejudice," a premise that is clung to without sufficient reason. Reason itself is thus unreasonable.[4]

Prophetically, Kant warned that "it is thus very harmful to plant prejudices, because they come back to plague those very people who themselves . . . have been the originators of these prejudices." While the cultural politics of reason were certainly useful at the time in combating even worse forms of prejudice in orthodox religion (the extremities of which in the Inquisition, Puritanism, etc., need no further rehearsing), it is arguable that in the last two centuries the prejudice of reason, the thoughtless presumption of its sufficiency, has come back to haunt the Enlightenment. To what degree have technical rationality, economic rationality, and the cult of science become the guardians of an uninvestigated orthodoxy and the guarantors of what Kant called our "immaturity," our inability to think for ourselves?[5]

What, after all, are these universalized abstractions—Reason, Nature, and, most notoriously, Common Sense—except kinds of rationalized divinity? This is the Enlightenment's strange polytheism. We bow and scrape to these gods to this day. Reason depends not on miracles but on an equally suspect form of revelation called "self-evidence." "We hold these truths to be self-evident," says our Declaration of Independence, and this assertion has always seemed philosophically good enough.[6] The language of self-evidence in our founding documents ought to seem to us just as suspect as the language asserting that we operate "under God." Why, after all, are there no ACLU legal suits to the Supreme Court objecting to the fact that schoolchildren are routinely taught to respect the notions of self-evidence, common sense, and clarity, all primary tenets in the Church of Reason? The evangelical Christian's faith in a God-made-incarnate stimulates the scorn of the reasonable, but somehow the appeal to the "self-evidence of inalienable human rights" is the stuff of a well-reasoned empiricism.

I cannot emphasize too strongly how powerful the authority of common sense still is among us. For example, liberal columnist Donald Kaul wrote that the federal court ruling against the teaching of intelligent design was a good thing because "it was a blow struck for common sense and clear thinking."[7] A blow for "clear thinking"? Let's be honest about it: clear thinking is anything that proceeds logically from *my* assumptions. It is a way of saying, "My assumptions are above question and do not need to be proven." Common sense and clear thinking are not terms that Kaul feels under any obligation to define or account for. They are, as ever, self-evident. The unfortunate consequence of such assumptions is that liberalism's "common sense" response to religious fundamentalism is little more than a blindness. Blindness for blindness.

Our values are not facts. They are not self-evident certainties. Neither the Bible nor science and not even the two together can make value certain. To argue that our most basic civic and ethical values are established by reasonableness or experience is just another form of what Thomas Paine called a "pious fraud." Benjamin Franklin, like Paine, believed in Reason as a temper in human conduct, but even Franklin suspected the scam. As he wrote in his autobiography, "So convenient a thing it is to be a *reasonable creature*, since it enables one to find or make a reason for everything one has a mind to do." It was something like this that Thoreau had in mind when he wrote in *Walden*, indicating pithily that in this as in most matters he had his own path to tread, "The commonest sense is the sense of men asleep, which they express by snoring" (216).

But the strangest consequence of the cult of Reason is in the effect it has had on public education. There the tradition of the Enlightenment has created not independent inquiry and "free thinking" but the strictest sort of respect for authority. For example, to return to the question of morals, it is true that we no longer teach Christian morality in our public schools, but neither do we teach Kantian morality. As Christians rightly complain, we teach nothing at all of morality to our children. This is so except that we teach by example the *morality of obedience to authority* whose first model for our children is the teacher and later the boss and the mass media. This is not obedience to church or obedience to a system of moral thought. It is *pure* obedience. The teacher says in essence, "What you should see in me is that I know how to obey, and you will learn to do the same." Our culture's only moral teaching, not lost on the young, is that we ought to be "successful," which finally means little more than "You must function within this system as it stands, you must not question it, and these are the advantages that you may expect to accrue to you if you learn to work well within it." All this in a context that is presumed to be secular, rational, free, and rooted in the good old Enlightenment.

But the dirty little secret is that Enlightenment has come full circle, and we are where we began: immature and unable to think for ourselves. In our commitment to obedience and success, and our sense that the two together are what we really mean by virtue, we are more like the ancient Romans than we know. We're like the Roman aristocracy measuring our virtue by our wealth. We're pagans rooting for the empire.

There is a passage in Donald Barthelme's wonderful short story "Me and Miss Mandible" that captures the real weight of the ethics of obedience.

> It may be that on my first trip through the schools I was too much under the impression that what the authorities . . . had ordained for me was right and proper, that I confused authority with life itself. My path was not particularly of my own choosing. My career stretched out in front of me like a paper chase, and my role was to pick up the clues. When I got out of school for the first time, I felt that this estimate was substantially correct, and eagerly entered the hunt. I found clues abundant: diplomas, membership cards, campaign buttons, a marriage license, insurance forms, discharge papers, tax returns, Certificates of Merit. (102)

Thus the true and unacknowledged secular morality of our schools. Obedience. *Sapere aude* ("Dare to think") be damned.

3.

The long failure of philosophical ethics to provide a foundation for morality led Nietzsche to conclude that an honest investigation of history would reveal that our moral concepts are in fact rooted in blood, cruelty, and unequal relations between debtors and creditors. For Nietzsche, all moral reasoning was question begging: we assume that there is a difference between the moral and the immoral and then set about looking for principles that allow us to distinguish between them. So, in God's absence, in the absence of any demonstrable moral principle, anything is possible. Anything is doable without ethical blame. In short, unlike Kant, Nietzsche concluded that morality would not survive thinking about it.

What does survive thinking are those things that are our values, our convictions, and our spirit, even though we have never known quite how to account for them. In the West, these convictions have a peculiar way of looking a lot like the Golden Rule, no matter how we try to obscure that fact. For instance, generations of readers of Kant's famous categorical imperative—"Act only on that principle which thou canst will should become a universal law"—have remarked on its similarity to Jesus's Golden Rule from the Sermon on the Mount—"Do to others whatever you would have them do to you" (Matthew 7:12). The Kantian imperative agrees with the Christian expression of the Golden Rule by demanding that we derive from our own self-interest a generalized concern for all human beings. In other words, both Kant and Jesus believed in a conscious and mutual recognition of the right of others to be treated kindly or, in Kant's phrase, as Ends. Jesus encouraged us to membership in the community of the church, Kant to citizenship in a Kingdom of Ends (which phrase itself echoes the biblical Kingdom of God). Most important, both gave force to the familiar complaint "How would you like to be treated like that?" What's "golden" about this ethic is its assertion of mutual concern over unfettered self-interest. This conviction has carried down even to Kant's descendants, philosophers like John Rawls, who argued that "each person [has] a right to the most extensive basic liberty compatible with a similar liberty for others." There's the glimmer of Jesus's Gold even in this most famously rational formulation. In short, in spite of its earnest efforts to distance itself from religion, philosophy has always found something deeply reasonable about Jesus's ethics.

Similarly for Marx, he could not have provided an ethical foundation to his critique of capitalism without revealing that he was, like Kant, far more dependent on Christian ethics than he himself understood. As John Ruskin might have chided Marx, "The laws that regulate the possession of wealth are unjust . . . but no socialism can effect their abrogation, unless it can abrogate covetousness and pride" (*Munera*: xxiv). In other words, for Ruskin there is an expressly spiritual problem at the heart of political economy. Or when Pope John Paul II, in his famously "unavoidable" encyclical on the "Culture of Death," wrote that it was an infamy to have "disgraceful working conditions, where people are treated as mere instruments of gain," he was not updating church thinking with a little halfhearted Marxism, and he was not mimicking Kant's admonition to treat people as ends, not means. He was speaking from Christianity's oldest and deepest moral tradition. It should also be clear that he was criticizing what passes as standard business practice under capitalism (even if John Paul could never quite bring himself to articulate that perception). *Capitalism cannot stop exploiting people as instruments of gain without becoming something other than capitalism.* Exploitation is the essence of its way of thinking. That is what it does. It finds unequal relations and exploits them. It's called a "business opportunity." Sometimes that means exploiting local labor, sometimes (and more often in these great days of "globalization") international labor. The church, of course, knows exactly why treating people as instruments of any kind is wrong: it has been revealed through the sacrifice and the historical ministry of Jesus. As St. Paul says in Philippians, "Do nothing out of selfishness or out of vainglory; rather, humbly regard others as more important than yourselves, each looking out not for his own interests, but everyone for those of others" (2:3).

In short, Marx could not answer the question "Why is capitalism bad?" without the unspoken assumption of Jesus's ethical revelation (although we ought always to remember that that ethics had its own sources in Hellenistic culture). Yet at its deepest levels Marxism *does* assume that capitalism is cruel, that exploitation is wrong, and that compassion for the suffering of people living under capitalism is the most important reason for revolution. This is why the first Marxist revolution happened in czarist Russia and not where it "should have," according to Marxist science—in an advanced capitalist culture. Marxist dogmatists have been scratching their heads in embarrassment about the Russian revolution for nearly a century. It shouldn't have happened there first. It should have happened in England where "objective conditions" were right. But Russians knew plenty about suffering under an age-old autocratic regime that routinely used cruelty to maintain inequality, and they knew plenty about indignation over the capriciousness of autocrats. The Russian peasant understood more about the real motivations of Marxism than the Marxist ideologues who would claim intellectual control of the revolution, would run the Communist Party after the revolution and become the peasant's next autocratic master. The great strategic error of Marxism was to imagine that it could achieve social justice through a mechanical understanding of the "necessary laws" of dialectical materialism, what came to be derisively known as "diamat," another word for Marxist dogma. "Capitalism must inevitably fall to the iron laws of its own internal contradictions," argued the Marxist theorists of the early twentieth century, dismissing the ethical authority of religion and replacing it with a perspective that assumed that political economy functioned like a sort of natural science of the "necessary." But Marxism was wrong to think that it had created a "science" (far less a natural science), and it was wrong to think that its hatred for the institution of the church required a hatred of spirituality as such. Most Russians certainly never did.

The idea that Marxism and Christianity share ethical/spiritual values is a large part of the meaning of Graham Greene's masterpiece *The Power and the Glory* (1940). Greene perfectly captures this idea in what is essentially a parable. The novel concerns a Marxist lieutenant who believes that he must kill a Catholic priest, even though the priest is a sort of harmless "whiskey priest," because the priest represents a corrupt institution that has conspired in the exploitation of his, the lieutenant's, people. The priest is a fugitive from this revolutionary, making his way among the peasants he once served, sleeping in their barns and fields. The revolutionary believes so fully in the necessity of the murder of the priest, this exercise of revolutionary justice, that he is even willing to kill his "own people," peasants, as hostages in order to get at the priest. But in the end, the drunken priest, representative of a corrupt church, and the idealistic revolutionary, who murders in the name of utopia, share the same spiritual values. The priest says to the revolutionary just before the lieutenant empties his revolver into his head, "You are a good man." This is not merely a pitiful gesture of moral largesse. It is a simple statement of recognition: I see what is in your heart, and it is good. Unhappily, in the fallen world in which they must act, neither can do anything but work against his own deepest and most ardent beliefs. They conspire together in their different ways to defeat a shared spiritual and ethical vision. Both the church and the revolution are corrupt, destructive, and murderous, but the desire for loving and just human relations is present nonetheless deep beneath their failed institutions.

I think that the difficulty that Kant and Marx experienced in distancing themselves from a Christian ethic is an indication of just how mistaken they were about the real meaning of the Christian era. Christianity was not merely another phase in the history of religious practice in the West; it was not just a collection of incredible stories believed only by child-minded adults. It was not just a pacifier of people abused under feudalism and capitalism obliging them to "accept their lot in life." Rather, it was nothing less than an apocalyptic moment in the history of ideas, in the history of ideas about *how to live*, a history they could not escape simply by wishing it dead and done (as both Kant and Marx did wish in their different ways). So, when Jesus said that he brought life and the end of the reign of death, he wasn't fooling the Jewish priests. When he spoke of the end of death, he meant the end of the social order administered by Jewish law. "Oh, *we're* death," thought the Pharisees, those who had most to lose in terms of social authority from the success of Jesus's revolution.[8]

It is Paul, in Romans, who understood the radical implications of Jesus's revolution best. For Paul, the Law, the Mosaic law, brought wrath, sin, and death. We were captive to the Law and thus captive to death. We were *servile* (a word to which I'll return) to a legality that hid cruelty and had little to do with the only commandment that mattered: you will love each other. Through Jesus the "letter" was made obsolete. The Pauline epistles to the early Christian communities make nonsense of the contemporary conservative conviction that a monument to the Ten Commandments ought to be sunk in the ground outside every public building, especially in front of courts of justice. The Ten Commandments—what Paul, after all, calls the "ministry of death"—are precisely what Christianity abolished. Paul writes in 2 Corinthians: "Now if the ministry of death, carved in letters on stone, was so glorious that the Israelites could not look intently at the face of Moses because of its glory that was going to fade, how much more will the ministry of the Spirit be glorious? For if the ministry of condemnation was glorious, the ministry of righteousness will abound much more in glory" (3). Moses's tablet was for Paul "the stone that causes stumbling" (Romans 9:32). We stumble to this day.[9]

Jesus was tried and executed for violations of Jewish law; he was killed for imagining that he was above the Law and thus above the priests who administered it. He was a revolutionary executed among revolutionaries. Consider Jesus's most basic rhetorical device: "It was said . . . but I tell you . . ."; "You have heard that it was said, 'You shall not commit adultery.' But I say . . . ." It is this rhetorical turn that contains his *revolutionary* intentions. For the incredulous Pharisees, who believed that "according to the Law" meant "according to God," this was nothing short of blasphemous. Apocalyptic, if it was allowed to stand. And so Jesus was killed.

Ironically, Jesus's crucifixion as an expression of the justice of Judaic law had the opposite effect, much to the chagrin of the Pharisees. Instead of being put to death by the Law, the Law itself was put to death, thus introducing a new moral order and through it a new sense of life. Jesus's ethical revolution is one in a series of revolutions over many centuries that will replace the rule of the general (the Law) with the primacy of the particular (the individual). Henceforth, it is the individual's experience as well as his feelings about those experiences that will count most. The new morality will be a morality of the individual heart. "For one believes with the heart and so is justified, and one confesses with the mouth and so is saved" (Romans 10:10).

The ardor of Marx's critique of capitalism is *transhistorically* the ardor of Jesus's ethical revolution. The human beings standing before you are not commodities even if they do sign contracts. They are not just abstract labor power. They are your brothers and sisters, and you *are* their keeper just as they are yours. Which is not to say that there is nothing of self-interest in the Golden Rule. "Do unto others as you would have them do unto you" absolutely implies that you know how you'd like to be treated. But rather than obliging the recognition of what you need from someone who is essentially a slave to you, the rule suggests the mutuality of community. We will see to each other's needs as equals.

This blend of Christian ethics and Marxist critique has of course been used forcefully for decades by Latin American liberation theology, but it was also a fundamental assumption of John Ruskin's essays on political economy, written in the 1860s. In these years, well before the publication of Marx's *Capital*, Ruskin argued that political economy as understood by Adam Smith and John Stuart Mill was wrong. Smith and Mill argued that political economy was a science concerned with the immutable laws of the accumulation of wealth understood as the accumulation of money. Ruskin, on the other hand, argued that political economy was impossible outside of the "conditions of moral culture." He wrote, "THERE IS NO WEALTH BUT LIFE." Labor under the unjust conditions of capitalism was "that quantity of our toil which we die in" (*Unto This Last*, 44). Capitalism was "the art of establishing the maximum inequality in our own favor" (48).

Opposed to the "mercantile economy" of the accumulation of money, of "mountains of gold," Ruskin proposed allowing people to make things that were beautiful and useful and finding their wealth in the making of life. His ideas led to the work of William Morris and the Arts and Crafts movement in England and the United States. To this day, the product of that work is admired, and the kind of work it represents—quality, durability, beauty, life—is longed for as a lost opportunity for an alternative economic and social order. Instead of a world of cooperation dedicated to a culture of life, we were left with the grim and fatal competitiveness overseen by the capitalist. For Ruskin, this was not simply the unfortunate victory of a bad idea; it was the death of a fundamental spiritual value. Quoting Alexander Pope, Ruskin concludes:

Yet, to be just to these poor men of pelf,
Each does but HATE HIS NEIGHBOUR AS HIMSELF

So, in spite of the title of former secretary of labor Robert Reich's recent book (*Reason: Why Liberals Will Win the Battle for America*), liberalism will not rise triumphant over a vanquished Christian fundamentalism because of its commitment to Reason. Nor should it. Reich believes that liberalism will triumph because it offers "better reasons." But reasons are only good or bad in relation to assumptions, and assumptions are finally what we mean when we speak of a culture's *spiritual* values. So, we don't need a renewed commitment to reason, we need a renewed commitment to justice rooted in our own oldest spiritual traditions (from Epicurus to Jesus to Ruskin to Marx and, as I will discuss in great detail later, our own Henry David Thoreau). That, at least, *ought* to win.

What both contemporary Christians and rational secularists have failed to understand is that justice is the heart of Western spirituality. Not the messiah, not the personage of a wrathful God, not the Commandments, not the Cult of the Virgin, and not the mysteries of the Knights Templar. The bottom line, if you will excuse me that expression, and what leftism of whatever stripe ignores at its own peril, is that this notion of justice on which every critique of authoritarianism depends is not demonstrable through any form of rational procedure. The left's critique always presupposes what can only be called an intuitive understanding of the Good. In the West, this Good is irrevocably tied to the fate of the Golden Rule even if, as I will argue later, the Golden Rule is for complex reasons no longer functional or available in our society. The tragedy is that in the present context the secular left believes that its advocacy of justice is independent of spirit, and the Christian right believes its spirituality is functional in the absence of justice. *The truth is that there is no spirit in the absence of justice and no justice that is not first spiritual.*

The problem is, of course, to know what "justice" means. For the moment, I will say that justice is not only the requirement to be equitable and fair, although that is certainly not irrelevant, nor is it simply the familiar Christian appeal to compassion. Most relevant, for me, is the strange and suggestive phrase in Hegel's lectures on the philosophy of religion. He speaks there of "the world in love." With this phrase in mind, the argument I will make in this book is that justice in its largest sense, and spirituality in its most important sense, has to do with what it means to be a human being, with what is fundamental to being human, and with the relation of humanity to a larger world that we call Nature or simply Being. Justice, as I will argue, is the *strength* of love in making a world that is deserving of human beings. The spirit of disobedience is not about a retreat from the world into Epicurus's famous garden where the individual can achieve the happiness of a "quiet mind." It is about the social refusal of the world as it stands and the reclaiming of it in the name of that most exasperated human quality, creativity. It is about human, as opposed to mercenary, world making. It is about, as Ruskin understood, wealth as life.

We have two choices before us, as a community. The first is the naked individualism of capitalism and property rights anarchists lost in an ethos unmoored to any sense of responsibility to others. This is Hegel's master/slave dialectic in which the master is so shaken at the thought of his own unreality that he enslaves the other as a perverse demonstration of his, the master's, triumphant individuality. The second choice is expressive of communalism and a deep respect for the dignity and worth of all others. It is Justice, and it is the only Culture of Life. Our problem has always been, in a culture so clearly committed to the first choice, to know how to understand and make real the second. That is the purpose of the chapters that follow. They are not proscriptive, and they do not constitute a Grand Plan. They are merely, in Thoreau's words, "the castles we build in the air and the beginning of the foundations we put under them."

Chapter 1

Imagination Dead Imagine

No trace anywhere of life, you say,
Pah, no difficulty there,
imagination not dead yet,
yes, dead, good,
imagination dead imagine.
—SAMUEL BECKETT

1.

Henry David Thoreau's *Walden* (1854) was not the work of a merely eccentric imagination. It was the work of a deeply spiritual and social imagination. As much as it sought to excuse itself as the conducting of "some private business," its real object was never anything less than the world. Thoreau's criticism of what the lives of his neighbors amounted to came out of his determination "to drive life into a corner, and reduce it to its lowest terms, and, if it proved to be mean, why then to get the whole and genuine meanness of it, and publish its meanness to the world" (66). Thoreau, like Nietzsche, sought to be the "bad conscience of his time" but not in order to sink into pessimism. Although Thoreau was convinced that his community was essentially dead in its own life, his efforts were meant not only to draw attention nihilistically to this desperate condition but to move beyond it, to revive the community, to *deliver* it. His work is an appeal to Life.

In our time as in Thoreau's, we live in lack. For Thoreau, inheritor through Ralph Waldo Emerson of European romanticism, it was the human imagination that had the power to revive the human world and restore it to spirit and life. In the present, the imagination has "copyright" stamped on it. It is owned, and it is expected to deliver a profit. Lost in characterizations of the world provided only by the mass media, we are spiritually impoverished, desperate, and capable of the most spectacular cruelties. The common usage by politicians and pundits of phrases such as "protecting our national interests," to which everyone nods sagely as if it were the most obvious and natural and blameless thing in the world, is in reality a piece of thoughtlessness, a deeply corrupt use of language, and a papering over of violence, spiritual failure, and death. This is to say nothing more than what George Orwell spoke of in his famous essay "Politics and the English Language." A debased use of language in "political speech and writing are largely the defense of the indefensible." The politician cannot overtly say, "I believe in killing off your opponents when you can get good results by doing so," but that is what our foreign policy has amounted to for the last fifty years at a minimum. As Harold Pinter put it in his acceptance speech for the 2005 Nobel Prize in Literature, "Language is actually employed to keep thought at bay. The words 'the American people' provide a truly voluptuous cushion of reassurance. You don't need to think. Just lie back on the cushion. The cushion may be suffocating your intelligence and your critical faculties but it's very comfortable."

We writers are not much less guilty, for we worry about what our agents can sell, what an editor is looking for, what an editor can get past his publisher, and what the good folks in marketing can make of it all. The writer is a "content provider" always being pressured to write to an industry standard. A utilitarian prose of "clarity" replaces personal style. As Thoreau complained nearly two hundred years ago, "in this part of the world it is considered a ground for complaint if a man's writings admit of more than one interpretation" (216).

Grim though this lack of spirit-as-imagination may seem, there is ample evidence that the political and spiritual longing for wholeness is nonetheless still present in our culture. Even in a debased condition, it is possible to know (speaking Platonically) that the Good exists. It is almost always unhappily the case, however, that the most dramatic examples of our desire for the Good, for spiritual wholeness, are also revealing examples of just how this desire is controlled, frustrated, and made subservient to the Market. Ironically, our desire for wholeness is almost always controlled not by some outside repressive and censorial source but by the artworks themselves. Our artworks don't need to be censored or repressed; they can be counted on to discipline themselves. They contain a "fascist within," as Michel Foucault puts it. Even the most minimal attention to what is happening in the work can reveal this self-disciplining, although ever fewer of us seem capable of or interested in this level of attention.

I'd like to look now at two examples of this self-disciplining as it has worked in two well-known, extraordinarily successful, and much misunderstood works of popular art: the movie *Office Space* and the novel *The Da Vinci Code*.

2.

The deeply American tradition of the slacker has its origins in American transcendentalism's encouragement to workers that they ought to relax into their work. "I loafe," says Whitman as if he were inventing a new virtue (not to mention an intriguing new spelling). "I idle. I linger." The thoughtless busyness of commerce frightened Thoreau and Whitman (when he wasn't seduced by the vision of its sheer undisciplined burning of energy) because it was clear to them how destructive of real human value it could be. As Thoreau writes ruefully of what was made of Walden Pond in the few years after he left his cabin,

Since I left those shores the woodchoppers have still further laid them waste, and now for many a year there will be no more rambling through the aisles of the wood, with occasional vistas through which you see the water. My Muse may be excused if she is silent henceforth. How can you expect the birds to sing when their groves are cut down? (132)

I think that most people are no less alarmed at what an all too industrious corporate capitalism is doing to our world in the present. The poor are ever greater in number, and more distant from social resources like health care, yet more invisible than ever to the affluent. Ice caps shrink and oceans rise, making cities like New Orleans, already below sea level, unlivable. Natural resources are depleted at an alarming rate. Fields of soybeans, with a productive life of less than a decade, eat into the Amazon forest like a colony of bacteria eating ever further into a living thing. Giant fisheries are depleted by factory trawlers whose only real product is profit for a very few at the expense of what once looked to be an infinite wealth of food for future generations. Warmer oceans spawn monster storms. Water tables in China, India, and the United States fall, threatening desertification and famine. Generally speaking, our "alarm" over these realities is in no way reflected in our daily conduct, which tends to look as if we're perfectly content to go on doing what we're doing, and our desperation is not so much "quiet" as deafening with the noise of automobiles, lawnmowers, and television sets. ("At least," we might complain, "Thoreau's Americans had a little 'quiet' in their desperation. I'd take a little quiet desperation at this point. It would be a real improvement.") But the potential for military, ecological, economic, and social disaster is clear to us all, or should be.

At the same time, people seem even *more* afraid of corporate capitalism's fragility. What frightens people is that it could all vanish tomorrow . . . to be replaced by what? What rough beast slouches our way now? Aren't there worse things than Wal-Mart? So, our social double bind is that even though we might hate it, we are anxious (worried sick!) about the possibility that it might all disappear! This anxiety is fed by the fact that all too frequently cracks in the edifice are obvious to all. The terrorist attack on the World Trade Center rocked our economy for two years. What would a dirty nuclear bomb exploded in Manhattan do? It would do more than shut down Wall Street for a couple of weeks. It would make the island of Manhattan, or neighborhoods therein, uninhabitable for decades. We're even anxious about our *own* ability to harm capitalism. What if we were all to decide to boycott Wal-Mart for one month? Mere rumors of a decline in "consumer confidence" send Wall Street plummeting. Consider that for a moment. One of the leading "realities" in our economic juggernaut is something called "consumer confidence." A measurement of something, you might say, but in the end *it is the most extraordinary kind of social fiction.* Yet when it goes south and the economy starts to follow, we suddenly see the president on TV urging us to consume with a sense of virtue, sure in the idea that the greatest patriotism is consumer patriotism, so we should all buy new refrigerators.[1] (No wonder we're a little mad about money. One month we're told to go shopping; the next we're blamed because we have no savings and are carrying monumental credit card debt.) So if vague intuitions about something called "consumer confidence" can cause havoc, what happens when people decide they've had enough and they're just going to stop shopping? Damn Wal-Mart. Damn McDonald's. Damn GM. (It may become clear in the next few years that GM has taken care of this damning all by itself through the epic folly of its wager on our endless appetite for trucks and SUVs.) Corporate America could vanish like the Soviet politburo, gone as if it never had been.

So, it ends up that what we're most afraid of is the collapse of the very thing that we're most opposed to. Out of fear, we remain committed to a system that has every appearance of heading for catastrophe. If the economy is dependent on consumption, but an economy of consumption is ultimately nonsustainable, then our efforts to sustain the economy are also efforts to sustain the certain arrival of disaster. It's like the Dave van Ronk song "Cocaine": "They say it'll kill me but they won't say when." Until they do tell us "when," we're going to just keep snorting, I guess.

While it would be wrong to dismiss the capacity of fear to stabilize our relationship to corporate reality, it would also be wrong to dismiss just how deep our *spiritual* dissatisfaction with the corporate life-world is. These two contrary impulses—hatred and fear, our civilized version of fight or flight—crystallize around *jobs*. Our problem with jobs is just what it was for Thoreau: What do we do with our human time? What do we exchange our lives for? We hate the corporate life-world for just this reason, because we hate giving it our lives, but we also fear the loss of our jobs and that fear keeps us dependent on them.

Recently, I was talking to one of my students, a young African American woman, who said to me, "I am poor. I have to work in order to go to school. But my job is with a debt collection agency. In order to live, I find myself doing the opposite of what I believe in. I must threaten poor people, old people, sick people, disabled people. I hate my job but I'm dependent on it." Then she looked up at me slyly. "Have you ever seen the movie *Office Space*?"

My students have all seen and all love *Office Space*, a movie by *Beavis and Butthead* creator Mike Judge. They love it for two powerful reasons. It's funny and it's hip. It's hip because they sense that it is subversive. *Office Space* is one of the few mainstream movies in which they feel they have been told the unvarnished truth about the nature of work. They believe that it presents the real world that waits for them. *Office Space* tells them, "In order to live, you will be asked to do what is no good, what is absurd, trivial, demeaning and soul killing." Thoreau couldn't have put it better. *Office Space* does not describe a world that they want to be part of, but at the same time they don't know how it can be avoided. They find the movie funny, but their laughter is nervous. They laugh because, ordinarily, no one talks about "jobs" in this way. Their parents don't. Politicians don't. Their teachers don't. Even their peers don't. The kind of work depicted in *Office Space* is supposed to be the good work, the creative work in our new information economy. It is the work we get to do because we sent all those nasty blue-collar jobs to Mexico and Southeast Asia. Yet here, in Judge's film, this work is depicted as deadening and humiliating, and young people know at some level that this is probably true, and if it's true, then what has been promised to them as "good" is also "death." So they laugh. And why not? It's a state of affairs worthy of Kafka. But there's also pleasure in this laughter because they have learned something about a contradiction in their world.

The contradiction has to do with the fact that these jobs are also the jobs dramatically at risk in the most recent international outsourcing of high-tech grunt work. So, they watch Lou Dobbs on CNN and worry about "exporting America," the betrayal of the future, their future. But then, perhaps, they think, "Hey, but those are the jobs in *Office Space*. Nobody wants those jobs. *I* don't want those jobs." It's crazy making. Nobody wants the jobs in the farm fields and slaughterhouses and suburban gardens that immigrant labor performs, and nobody wants factory work, so we send all that to the third world, and now nobody wants to sit and write computer code in a corporate carrel. Is it possible that what we're discovering is that we don't want jobs at all? What we really want is to do, as *Office Space*'s hero Peter claims, absolutely nothing? Are we a nation of slackers after all? Do we all want to go and "loafe" with Whitman and Thoreau?

These are the quandaries that Mike Judge explores in *Office Space*. He recognizes the conflict between a general hatred for the nature of work and a companion fear that it might disappear. Peter, our protagonist, represents hatred for work. His pals, Michael and Samir, represent fear that it might disappear, never mind how much they hate it.

PETER: What if we're still doing this when we're fifty?

SAMIR: Would be nice to have that kind of job security.

The feelings about work that Judge gives to his characters have not been so broadly and powerfully expressed since Paul Goodman's *Growing Up Absurd* (1960). We recognize Peter's despair as our own, or we see it with dread as our future. How else to explain the way this movie has resonated with its young audience?

PETER: Every single day of my life has been worse than the day before it. So that means that every day that you see me, that day is the worst day of my life.

Peter is relieved of his anxiety about losing his job when he is accidentally left in a state of total relaxation after his therapist has a heart attack before withdrawing him from a hypnotic state. Peter is suddenly and weirdly transformed. He doesn't care about his job, paying bills, or much of anything else. But there's something peculiar about his new, relaxed state. He doesn't have the zombie-like qualities that movies usually attribute to hypnosis. Rather, he seems mellow. He seems *stoned*. Judge is plainly making an allusion to the 1960s process of "feeding your head" or getting "experienced" as a preamble to dropping out of the corporate rat race.

Now, the power of these images of loathing for work and getting stoned and doing nothing may be so central to the experience of the movie that it doesn't matter what other narrative logic is present. What we remember of the movie is the awfulness of the work space, and the convincing awfulness of the boss (Bill Lumbergh, played perfectly by Gary Cole), and the battered and grotesque awfulness of the most abject victim, Milton, who stands as a moral exemplar to us all: this could be you! Nonetheless, Judge, like most Hollywood filmmakers, seems as much terrified as inspired by his own social vision. In most ways, the film's narrative logic demands that it back away from its own insights. And furiously backpedal it does.

Hatred of job, stoned vision, and slacker freedom firmly established, Judge begins to retreat in earnest when Peter has an interview with the "Bobs," two outside consultants brought in to downsize Initech's payroll. Peter has confessed to them that he does "maybe fifteen minutes" of real work each week. He then expresses an about-face on his own desire to do "nothing at all." It's not that he's a slacker. He simply lacks that hoary old capitalist incentive to work: profit motive.

PETER: It's not that I'm lazy. It's that I just don't care. It's a problem of motivation, right? Now if I work my ass off and

Initech ships a few extra units, I don't see another dime. Where's my motivation?

Judge here retreats from what at first appeared an uncompromising opposition to the corporate world. The movie seems not to believe in its own most fundamental social convictions, odd as that should sound. Peter doesn't want freedom, apparently. He doesn't want creativity or personal autonomy. He wants "profit sharing." Are we supposed to imagine that the horror of life under boss Bill Lumbergh all goes away if we get profit sharing?

It would be nice to think that this is some sort of false step or illogic in the film. Unfortunately, it is merely a familiar betrayal. After an early moment of truth telling, we are now firmly on the road to a happy ending, all reconciled to the world as it is.

The next step in this process of retrenchment in the comfort of the established order concerns the nerdy white boys posing as high-tech gangstas. With the rhythms of rap in the background, Peter, Michael, and Samir concoct a plot to steal money from Initech by planting a virus in the payroll software that will transfer fractions of pennies to a secret account (accessible through Peter's ATM?!—that sounds foolproof). This money will allow them to live free of Initech forever. Peter tries to justify his scam by explaining that he has had a vision, an epiphany:

> PETER: It's not just about me and my dream of doing nothing. It's about all of us together. . . .

But as Peter's girlfriend (Joanna, played by Jennifer Aniston) points out, it's just stealing. He's just saving his own skin while the rest of us rot. He's just another corporate criminal as even he seems to understand in the film's biggest laugh line.

> SAMIR: I'm not going to do anything illegal.

> PETER: Illegal? Samir, this is America!

But the ultimate betrayal that the film has to offer is, strangely, generic. The audience, especially its young audience, is consistently wondering as it watches, "Just how seriously do I have to take this movie?" At a certain point, with the introduction of Jennifer Aniston as Joanna and the beginning of the film's romantic angle, Judge makes it clear that they don't have to take any revolutionary theses seriously, the "Lord, it feels good to be a gangsta" rap is all hype, just as sold out as gangsta rap in general is these days, and what we really have here is a profitable Hollywood romantic comedy. In complete and abject submission to the usual polite formulas and proprieties, Peter explains at the film's noxious conclusion: "I may never be happy with my job. But I think that if I could be with you that I could be happy with my life. I've been a real asshole, but if you can give me a shot, I . . . ." Joanna then hushes him with a kiss, much as leading ladies have done to their Hollywood beaus for decades. For some of us who actually remember seeing a film or two with real subversive intent (Melvin Van Peeble's *Putney Swope* comes to mind), this scene provokes the nastiest welling up in the esophagus of the mother of all acid reflux: cop-out! Betrayal!

This betrayal is confirmed at the film's end when Peter resolves the problem of work by getting a job in the happy world of the construction worker, the carefree and curiously prosperous life of the unskilled laborer. Judge romanticizes the working stiff. Peter can just shovel crap, eat lunch with Joanna, and shoot the bull with his pal Laurence. That's happiness.

PETER: Makin' bucks, gettin' exercise, workin' outside.

LAURENCE: Fuckin' A.

PETER: Fuckin' A.

The cynicism of multimillionaires like Mike Judge and Jennifer Aniston telling us to find happiness with a shovel is monstrous. All of the trust generated early in the film through damning depictions of work go spiraling away in disgust. The only answer the film provides to its big question, "What should we do about alienation in work?" is "Nothing—give up; find a way to conform."

As I said earlier, it may be that the film's real impact is in its potent images of work and that the rest is irrelevant. But the narrative logic is there. At best it serves to so muddy the issues that the viewer is left confused. What does this film think? Is it suggesting that anyone actually do anything? Should we quit the jobs we hate? No. It suggests that you slink back to work like Michael and Samir, and if the pain gets really bad, just crank the gangsta rap up a notch. Or you can join the happy, healthy world of unskilled labor, where your millionaire girlfriend sits beside you as you eat your lunch from a pail. Or you can fix it all the American way by cheating, embezzling, and scooting off to some Caribbean island, as Milton does, to do that ugly American thang and complain about the piña coladas. But do something wild like figure out what a real human life might look like? Nah. The worldview of *Office Space* allows corporate capitalism to go on with its monstrous and sterile "creativity," while its subjects remain merely abject. Dead.

For all its glee in satirizing corporate reality and for all its Luddite fantasies of beating laser-jet printers with a baseball bat, *Office Space* is finally a movie that does not encourage us to do anything. It certainly does not encourage us to disobedience. If there is a social or spiritual conviction that at some point laid claim to its creators, they were certainly not faithful to it. It is for that reason not just a bad movie, or a hypocritical movie, or a sell-out movie: it is a little spiritual defeat. It is a movie without hope. Like the conservative in Ralph Waldo Emerson's essay "The Conservative," *Office Space* argues pessimistically that "the order of things is as good as the character of the population permits" (*Essays and Lectures*, 182). The present order of things becomes irrational, like a notion of a common fate, "fate in dread degrees," as Emerson puts it. Fatal. "The Conservative assumes sickness as a necessity" (*Essays and Lectures*, 185). For an authentic spiritual thinker of the American grain like Emerson, mentor to the disobedient Thoreau, all authentic spirituality is the work of the "private heart." *Office Space* establishes its convictions and its credibility through the truths of the private heart, Peter's soul searching. But it ends in the necessity of work. It ends in despair.

Fuckin' A.

3.

The philosopher Paul Ricoeur speaks of faith not as something that one has or that one asserts into the world, nor is it the willingness to say that you believe in the unbelievable. Faithfulness, for Ricoeur, is our response to that which "claims" us. And so perhaps we can say that the creators of *Office Space* were "claimed" by a vision of human wholeness, just as Jesus, Marx, and Thoreau were before them. If so, they failed to maintain faith with that which had claimed them. In their failure, they join themselves to the fate of capitalism. Ricoeur called capitalism a "failure that cannot be defeated." This failure is not solely a matter of social and economic justice, although it is certainly that. It is first, if not foremost, a spiritual failure. All the other ways in which it is unjust follows from that fact. Let me put it this way: what does capitalism (especially in its virulent "free market" form) project into the future as its spiritual heritage? With every passing decade, it becomes clearer that its spiritual heritage is a human and natural world laid waste. In strange ways almost too frightening to contemplate, our dominant Christian culture, more like David Koresh's Branch Davidians than it knows, anticipates this "world laid waste" as if it were a good, or at least inevitable, thing. It is, for some, the apocalypse predicted by Revelations. The alliance of corporate/military rationalism with Christian fundamentalism is the death of hope for what is deserving of our love.

So, it seems to me that one of the things that calls to us most urgently, if we are to oppose this version of the "end-time," is that we, too, need to know those things that are most "fundamental" to us. What are the things that have "claimed" us and to which we owe faithfulness? What do we invest with the force of our caring? How vulnerable is it? How deserving is it? Who would join us in loving it and in committing it to the care of the future? When we have discovered those things, we need to stop living through fear, as if we were part of a conspiracy against ourselves. We need to acknowledge that which has "claimed us" by advancing, as Thoreau put it, "confidently in the direction of [our] dreams" and endeavoring "to live the life which [we have] imagined" (215).

The opportunity to maintain faith in "that which claims you" does from time to time pop up for us in prominent and sometimes spectacularly prominent ways. The much-lauded novel *The Da Vinci Code*, for example, is a work of popular fiction that has somehow also become an object around which the most fantastic spiritual ambitions have circled. At one level it is simply a pulp novel about a detective hero (Harvard "symbologist" Robert Langdon), a murder, an encrypted message from the murder victim, and a freight load of arcane and sensational speculations about secret societies (Opus Dei, the Knights Templar, the Priory of Sion) and their mischievous and malicious roles in world history. But at another level the novel seeks to educate its readers about the (factual) role of Gnosticism in the early Christian church and the (dubious) erotic relationship between Jesus and Mary Magdalene. This narrative line culminates in the notion that the Holy Grail is actually a metaphor for the holy bloodline created by Jesus and Magdalene through a daughter, Sarah, and perpetuated in the descendants of the Merovingian kings. Thus the novel's most sensational suggestion (aside from fantasies about Jesus and Mary *in flagrante*) is that people still walk the Earth with the messianic DNA.[2]

In spite of all this sensation, I think that what *The Da Vinci Code* has created should be of interest to us, but its interest is not in the fact that, as his many fans argue, Dan Brown is right about Da Vinci or the infamies of the Catholic Church or powerful secret societies or the real role of Mary Magdalene as apostle and lover to Jesus. The publishing phenomenon of *The Da Vinci Code* is important as a symptom of what is lacking in our culture, what people are, yes, *seeking,* and how the potential social power of that seeking is managed by the larger culture. *The Da Vinci Code* is important because it is the expression of a desire for a spirituality that cannot be had within the confines of the institutionalized church. More simply yet, it is the popular expression of a desire for a kind of meaningfulness to life that is missing for most of us. And, certainly, it is the scandalous expression of a willingness to be disobedient to achieve the heretical end of a salvation outside the confines of the church. Through this novel, we express our fundamental disgust with our institutionalized lives, and we suggest shocking things that we might previously have imagined were unsayable. The novel offers the unexpected opportunity to flee the dominant culture of Truths-That-Make-No-Sense into the Secret, the Unsayable, and the True.

From my point of view, there's nothing wrong with imagining that there is something fraudulent about the way our lives are ordered, and there's nothing wrong with wanting to go beyond the illusory in order to know the truth. Beyond the scandal and the sensation and the heavy-handed fiction, it is this assumption of our shared feeling of spiritual fraud and the assumption that we're willing to think heretically in order to escape that fraud that makes Brown's deepest appeal to his readers. Brown promises a kind of liberation to us, and our eagerness to take up his offer says something revealing about our spiritual as well as our political condition.

In other words, the interest in Gnosticism and alternative forms of Christianity (like the Gospel of Thomas) that *The Da Vinci Code* has stimulated holds the possibility for a kind of *seriousness* that few other aspects of popular culture can claim. Unfortunately, as with most "serious" matters in mass culture, the opportunity to have real consequence is abolished in the same moment that it is extended. The *Code* and its many commentaries offer two contradictory possibilities. It is the expression of an authentic longing, and it is the incredulous insistence that we can't really mean what we seem to be saying. To really mean this business about the hidden history and the unacknowledged malice of the Catholic Church, about the relationship of a secret society like Opus Dei to the administration of the federal government, is too scary to be taken entirely seriously. So our anxiety about really meaning any of this stuff, seriously proposing the critique as an alternative to the religio-corporate present, is immediately effaced by the assurance that—not to worry!—it's just a pulp fiction. It's just a scandal-commodity. It obliges its audience to nothing more than a familiar and ephemeral enthusiasm, and a willingness to stimulate a "market" (in this case, the ever-beleaguered book market that staggers from year to year only on the strength of Tolkien reprints, the next Harry Potter adventure, novelistic sensations like the *Code*, and tell-alls by disgraced politicians, celebrities, and baseball players on steroids).

Let's take, as an instance of the *Code*'s ambiguity, the revelations about Mary Magdalene and her sexual relationship with Jesus. She represents, on the one hand, a critique of the church's misogynist and patriarchal past. Moreover, she offers not only a secret history but also a secret and erotic spirituality. But she also represents the scandalous and merely lurid idea that she and Jesus did the nasty together. Which option is it that has the greater power to explain the interest in a book like *The Da Vinci Code*? In some ways, the two aspects work together, entertaining and instructing, as Horace puts it in his *Ars Poetica*. But I would contend what Horace never suggested. *The entertainment makes the instruction possible, but it also destroys its meaning.* *The Da Vinci Code* makes political and spiritual notions of great potential power broadly available but only with the implicit assurance that these notions will not be made real. These theses will never be nailed to a church door. It's the cultural equivalent of computer code on a CD that makes it possible to play the CD but not to reproduce it. Cultural meaning is created but only on the condition that its impact will be carefully managed and limited.

Let me put this another way. The authentic social function of the imagination operating through the arts is to submit to destruction the standing assumptions of the moment but then to redeem that destruction through a process of rebuilding and reimagining. That's what art does. It destroys and redeems, wipes the slate clean and then re-creates. But a work like *The Da Vinci Code* does just the opposite. It first holds out the possibility of a vast reimagining only in order to betray it through the reestablishment of the familiar (in this case, the jaded world of the bourgeois scandal-commodity). In short, it suggests redemption without ever having the courage to destroy anything. In the end, its real *formal* function is to reassure, to console, to make one comfortable not with the new and blasphemous but precisely with the most undifferentiated familiar: the juicy pulp of the pleasure-commodity.

Works like *The Da Vinci Code*, I suppose, do us the favor of encouraging us to doubt the ancient magical thinking of the institutional church without dismissing the human purpose of spirituality. Unfortunately, Dan Brown is little concerned with helping us to find the reasonable core of Christianity's promise beneath the accretions of dogma and myth. In many ways, Brown's charges against the Catholic Church were standard Reformation complaints. The church is legalistic and hypocritical and rank with pagan mythology and ritual. Protestantism argued for a return to the scriptural beliefs of the primitive church in the first Christian communities. But, departing from Protestantism, Brown does not seek a return to the authentic. Rather, he replaces one occult crust with another. Gone is the magical thinking behind the virgin birth and Jesus as deity. In its place is the New Age fantasy of Mary Magdalene as the "eternal feminine" bearer of the holy bloodline. The scandalous possibility that "intelligent people want to know" is "do blood relatives of Jesus walk among us?" But neither option allows access to a faith that is not also foolish.

In a word, *The Da Vinci Code*'s seriousness is deeply unserious. Its promise of truth is broken in the moment it is made. The culture's habit of *finding "seriousness" acceptable only if offered by people who are finally not serious* is yet another way that our culture makes certain that nothing alarming will come of our newfound interest in heretical ideas. At moments like these, everybody—writers, journalists, readers, the whole lot—fall over themselves to confess failure. On the other hand, this is all only as it should be in a culture that believes that it can learn about theology by reading a pulp novel.

4.

The word *sacred* should frighten us. If the sacred is figured in a once-and-for-all-time revelation rooted in a fixed reading of a sacred text, that is a scary thing. Millions of people have suffered and died in the last two thousand years—Hindus, Jews, Christians, Muslims, and all the sects between—for such a fixed understanding of the sacred. A faith in the absolute Truth of a sacred text, or of one interpretation of that text, always has the effect of creating an Other, the Unbeliever. The apostate to the Truth. The unfaithful. The Infidel. Yet behind this "frightening" and bloody purpose is a very human thing that only a fool or a rationalist would say humans don't need. This "human thing" is the permanent process of seeking the sacred through *revealing* what is hidden. It is an ever ongoing and indefinite process of understanding and interpretation. While it is all too unhappily clear that there is a large and growing community for the sacred as fixed Truth, as our many fundamentalist sects demonstrate daily (often with explosives strapped to their bodies), it is not so clear that there is a community for the sacred as ongoing revelation. What the Imagination and its traditions argue is that the world is never finally sacred. God's Kingdom never finally arrives, and the desire for a City on the Hill in perfect correspondence with faith is demonstrably as dangerous as the Stalinist desire for a perfected communist society. What never leaves, for the Imagination, is the open and creative desire for the sacred, if for no other reason than that that is the best way to show how fallen, corrupt and damaged the present is.

So, Dan Brown has done us the favor of showing that, yes, there is potentially a large and powerful community (as opposed to an audience of consumers) open to the idea of rereading and rearticulating what the sacred will stand for in our historical moment. At its best, the *Code* is a book whose primary desire is to make the world sacred again and to redeem the world from fraud. But we are not the first generation to discover that the world has been desecrated or, literally, desacralized. Unfortunately, our way of confronting a desacralized world, as represented by *Office Space* and *The Da Vinci Code*, is self-defeating from the beginning. But then neither *Office Space* nor *The Da Vinci Code* is a work of art.

As I have argued, authentic works of art do not make an acceptance of the world as it stands an assumption of the work. For example, Shakespeare's *Hamlet* is also a work about a world that has lost its sacred meaning. Unlike Brown's *Code*, it is also a work that gives direction for the resacralizing of the world. It is also, I'll emphasize, a great work of art because of the power with which it destroys and then redeems. *Hamlet* is a work that is familiar to most of us, even if only through one movie version or another. The character Hamlet, like his creator Shakespeare, is a "culture hero." Hamlet has been and remains a literary rock star whose continued relevance not even the PC police question, (fictional) Dead White Male though he may be. Yet the play's very familiarity and the easy assumption of its "greatness" is almost a guarantee that no one will think about it beyond acknowledging its greatness. And certainly few of us would imagine that it provides an important explanation of our spiritual fate for the last five hundred years. But I think it does.

Hamlet assumes a world that was, in the very recent past, sacred. The world as ruled by Hamlet's father, the murdered king, was one in which duty followed not from authority (the law or mere brute compulsion) but from love. Hamlet owed duty to his father, just as Hamlet's friend Horatio maintained loyalty to Hamlet, not because he was in some way obliged to but because he loved his father. Hamlet's father earned this love and earned loyalty and duty not because he was the king but because he was just. This is a Christian ethic at work. In Christianity, Love replaces the Law at the apex of a community. What makes the Christian world sacred is the establishment of a human community based on love, justice, and an obligation to honor justice through conscience and duty.

All this is destroyed by Claudius, the king's brother, who murders Hamlet's father out of *desire*. Claudius desires power, wealth, and the body of the queen, Hamlet's mother, the concupiscent Gertrude. With Claudius's ascension to the throne, duty is gone. Obligation out of fear of the consequences is all that remains of the community. When Claudius asks Rosencrantz and Guildenstern, Hamlet's friends since childhood, to betray Hamlet by turning him over to death at the hands of the English, they obey only because they know that not to obey is to accept death for themselves. This is a world that has lost its sanctity; the Christian sanctity of love has been lost to mere authority. The world has been made profane and merely political. The death of Hamlet ushers in the world of

Machiavelli where duty has no merit beyond fear and a desire for personal gain or simple survival. Hamlet intuits the sinfulness of this moment in his perception that the world has been alienated from its true self. Denmark is no longer Denmark. It is rotten. It is a corpse, just as the king is a corpse. Humans are now only their bodies, food for worms. The spirit is dead.[3]

The loss of a world that functions through a sense of duty earned by justice and rooted in love leads Hamlet to doubt the very worthiness of existence itself. Hence his morbidity. The question of the worth of being becomes quite serious. To be, or not to be. His flesh itself is "sullied." He laments the laws against "self-slaughter." The earth has become a "sterile promontory," and the human body, God's temple, is something fattened for maggots. There is no comedy here and no hope. Comedy is something for a world that turns out whole in the end. *Hamlet* announces the death of comedy. The play's only truly typical comic character, Polonius, meets a most untypical end, murdered meaninglessly by Hamlet. Polonius is nothing more than "guts" for lugging into the neighbor room. Death to the funny man.

Hamlet's drama, although he rarely understands it in these terms, is about his effort to make his world sacred again. Unfortunately, Hamlet's adolescent impulses lead him in the wrong direction. His desire to avenge his father's death through the murder of Claudius is inappropriate, because revenge commits him not to his father's Christian ethic but to the tribal ethic of an eye for an eye. To avenge his father's murder will not restore his father's spiritual reign; it will only further alienate it. Moses cannot meaningfully confront Machiavelli. This is Hamlet's greatest error.

Of course, this error leads to a conclusion that is nothing short of apocalyptic. But it is an apocalypse that is also potentially redemptive. The question is, What survives the general slaughter? In *Hamlet*, the final scene is a brutal leveling of all of the major characters. Only Horatio survives and with him something of the murdered king's ethic of loyalty based on justice. But the martial Fortinbras, a minor character who arrives on stage only in the play's very last moment, also survives. Fortinbras (his name means, literally, "strength in arms") clearly cannot be about the restoration of the king's ethic. Fortinbras is at one with the Machiavellian Claudius. One can only fear for Horatio's safety in a world ruled by the rash Fortinbras.

If this is the case, if it is in the end Claudius's ethic that survives through Fortinbras, where is Shakespeare's redemptive gesture? How does he attempt to figure a renewed sacred? Are we condemned to a future based only on the irrational compulsions of the law and the fear of authority? Are we to imagine that Shakespeare really *welcomes* the dawning of a world based only on calculation of self-interest?

The answer to this question is right before us. As Hamlet says, "The play's the thing." It is the nature of the artwork itself, the hitherto unknown aesthetic power of the artwork *Hamlet*, that most restores a sense of the meaningfulness of the world. If religion, whether tribal or Christian, has failed to hold the human world together, has failed to provide a sense of human meaningfulness, it is up to the work of art, *Hamlet*, with its deep commitment to the individual, the astonishingly personal voice and vision of the artist Shakespeare, the aesthetically delivered indignation at the idea of a world lacking justice, the great longing for wholeness that is expressed in the formal beauty of the work itself, these things begin to rearticulate the human world as something more than a host for worms. It is the beginning, as Harold Bloom has famously said of Shakespeare, of the invention of the human. It is now a critical commonplace among Shakespeare critics that, as Anne Barton writes in her introduction to the Penguin edition of *Hamlet*, "*Hamlet* marks a cultural and historical watershed: the moment when 'modern' man—sceptical, complex, self-lacerating, uncertain of his relationships with other people and with a possibly bogus world of heroic action—achieved artistic embodiment" (17).

What is not so clear is that *Hamlet* is also the beginning of a postinstitutional spirituality. If Christian ethics have been defeated by the Claudiuses and Fortinbrases and Machiavellis of the world, who have substituted for morality mere rational manipulation and calculation of self-interest, it was up to Shakespeare and the work of art to show the way to make the world sacred again. But this "making-sacred" did not happen through a return to Christianity. The Christian worldview was defeated metaphysically by Reason, and it was defeated spiritually by pragmatics, by rational and political self-interest. In the end, there is no undoing Claudius's betrayal. But the spiritual kernel in Christianity—its insistence on a human world ruled by love and justice—became the inheritance of artists and thinkers like Shakespeare who would actually work against the grain of victorious rationality in order to maintain the human world as a sacred place. *Hamlet* is a spiritual celebration in the face of the terrible. A god dances through it.

There is something "perverse," as Slavoj Žižek would put it, about the reclaiming of the spirit that Shakespeare accomplishes. Shakespeare betrays Christianity in order to maintain its core. For Žižek, "religious betrayal" is performed by those who "love me enough to betray me" (19). Shakespeare's betrayal of Christianity is therefore religious: it is "betrayal out of love." Žižek writes:

> I respect you for your universal features, but I love you for an X beyond these features, and the only way to discern this X is betrayal. I betray you, and then, when you are down, destroyed by my betrayal, we exchange glances—if you understand my act of betrayal, and *only* if you do, you are a true hero. (19)

Jesus, confronted by the destructive betrayal of Machiavellian self-interest and political calculation, welcomes the religious betrayal of Shakespeare and exchanges with him this loving glance.

5.

In short, the spiritual content to be found in art is not in its "themes," and it is not in the apparent tragedy of the plot. It is in the formal qualities of the work itself. And so, closer to home than *Hamlet*, Ang Lee's recent and notorious *Brokeback Mountain* is perceived by some as good because it displays the liberal virtues of tolerance, and by others as good because its ending, like *Hamlet*'s, is tragic. But I would contend that the film is spiritually alive in ways that works like *The Da Vinci Code* cannot imagine and that few viewers of the film suspect. In fact, contrary to all critical commentary that I have seen, director Ang Lee is much less interested in his "gay cowboys" than most of us imagine. If the film is really about what its critics have claimed it is about—"forbidden passion" and "the anguish of unfulfilled love" that "hits you like a shot in the heart"—then it is a trite movie. After all, Lee himself has said, "I just wanted to make a love story." (To which I can only respond, "Dear God!")

What I was most impressed by in the film was how persistently it refused to gloat about its social virtues and refused to be bowed by the logic of tragedy. Rather, it confronts the oppressiveness of a destructive society—the murder of gay men; the despair of working-class life—through a remarkable rethinking of cowboy stoicism and an insistence on . . . *joy*.

It is to the film's credit that the brutal murder of Jack Twist is not its true climax. The murder is dramatically obligatory, perhaps, because of the bigoted requirement that gay love must be depicted as tragic in the end. (We're in a place now where we'll put up with looking at same-sex naughtiness on the screen, but in the end we still expect it to be tragic, painful, and destructive.) As a consequence, the range of our possible reactions to this film is limited to "That's so sad" or "Gee, we're such a fucked-up society" or, disturbingly, "Rural people are cruel and violent."

Curiously, for me the dominant emotion of the film was not sadness. It was joy. Pleasure. We see this joy in two consistent ways throughout the film. First, in the gorgeous and deeply pleasurable cinematography of brilliantly angled shots of sheep flowing over mountains, water flowing over rocks, and horses climbing among trees. I was reminded of the kind of counterpoint that Akira Kurosawa used to achieve in his samurai movies like *Kagemusha* when the beauty of the flowing lines of horses, men, and colorful banners argued against the reality of what they were doing—preparing for slaughter. Critics have commented on the beauty of the cinematography in *Brokeback*, but it's as if that beauty were somehow separate from the film's meaning. It's an extra, a bonus, an add-on. There's the sad story of the cowboys, and then, by the way, there's the visual grandeur. But the visual rhetoric of a film should be integral to its drama. In *Brokeback*, the visual denies the social, and it especially denies the easy appeal to sadness. This movie glories in what it sees, as well it should.

Second, there is the consistent joy in acting, especially Heath Ledger's performance as Ennis. Again, most critics abstract the acting from the film. It's a great performance, but the quality of the performance has little to do with what the film "means." But what I find most wonderful about Ledger's performance is its excess. It is in excess of dramatic requirements. His performance itself becomes the focus of interest in the film, and it is deeply pleasurable. I would also suggest that the joy/pleasure of Ledger's performance is always arguing against the film's social themes and therefore against its nihilism. It's as if Lee is saying, "How can this story be sad if there's so much beauty in this face, this voice, this performance?" But looking at the film in this way requires us to do something we're not very good at. It requires us to imagine that it is an artifice, something made up, and not merely a reflection of "reality."

Admittedly, the stereotypical "depressing" conclusion is present. In the end, Ennis is impoverished, broken-hearted, without prospects, and living in a seedy trailer. But this sadness is what the film seems most determined to deny. Instead, Lee piles affirmation on affirmation. It's not the trailer that matters but what can be seen out the window. It's not Ennis's lost love that matters but his affirmation of his love for his daughter. The thing that has gone completely unaccounted for in this film is just how *happy* Ennis seems at the end. Lee achieves not only a transvaluation of cowboy stoicism, lifting it to spectacular social breadth, but he also achieves what Nietzsche called *amor fati*, love of fate. In the end, Ennis does not merely passively endure; he embraces the entirety of his experience. As Nietzsche put it, "The task is so to live that you must *wish* to live again." Ennis embodies this affirmation. As bad as it was, he'd do it again. Eternally, if need be.

41

And so this film behaves as it should. It refuses to confirm nihilism, tragedy, and despair, in spite of the facts. It asserts its right to live quite irresponsibly outside of all social themes in the great Nietzschean "yea to life." All the while that it builds its tragic plot, it is dancing in plain view, in love with its own visual and performative powers. When we walk away from the film and say that we liked it, we are responding to these pleasures although we speak mostly of the film's themes, as if we'd feel guilty about pleasure when there are such *serious* problems at hand.

Most important, Lee's "yea to life" is perhaps a more dangerous antagonist to oppression of whatever stripe than building a political movement. Beauty is dangerous and a challenge to oppression, but in a way that social reform movements can hardly imagine. That is because most social reform movements are rational (change this law, protect these people, call in the feds) and not finally spiritual. *Brokeback*, like *Hamlet*, is dangerous because it creates a kind of *demand* (both individual and social) that cannot be limited. *Brokeback* does not argue for more and better laws to prevent homophobia and rural poverty. It is not the film of an activist. The squalor of life in the High Plains is consistently refused by the film's own obsessive need for cinematic pleasure. Ang Lee is impatient with his own social themes, to which, by my reading, he is in the end nearly indifferent. He is finally only really interested in creation, in the pleasure of *making*. It is in this way that he is most spiritual and most unlike the world around him. Unlike the director of *Office Space*, Lee does not betray his expressed beliefs. Rather, he keeps faith magnificently with a belief that is nearly secret to his audience.

The problem that I see in the sort of spiritual seeking typical of Dan Brown's *Da Vinci Code* and its obsession with the mysteries and arcana of ancient Christianity is that it misses the point. It's seeking what isn't lost. There is a spirituality of critical importance to us all, and it is right before us. But we don't see it because we call it secular. Students are told that "*Hamlet* is a 'great work of art' written by a man of 'genius,' and we should learn to 'enjoy and appreciate' it." But who suggests that it is a spiritual opportunity?

Who would say that its real purpose is spiritual, even apocalyptic: to provide an *intensity* of experience that will allow its audience to willingly submit the world to destruction, to apocalypse, in order in that *ecstatic moment* to experience the arrival of a world made new? The work of art seeks to create conviction. It seeks an ever-renewable revelation. Is that a model to offer to high school students and art appreciation classes in our public schools? I'd like to think so, but there's probably not a school board in the country that would agree with me.

Chapter 2

Beyond the Golden Rule

I tell you, no virtue can exist without breaking these
ten commandments. Jesus was all virtue, and acted
upon impulse, not from rules.
> —WILLIAM BLAKE, *The Marriage of Heaven and Hell*

1. ·

In Shakespeare's *Hamlet*, perhaps the most conspicuous
assumption about the state of the world is that the reign
of an ethic of universal love rooted in duty to a just father is ended.
Clad in his "inky cloak," Hamlet is not only proto-Goth (his
favorite bands? The Cure and Depeche Mode) but also proto-
Nietzschean. Hamlet is the returned Jesus bringing the bad news
this time: my father is dead, and he won't be back. ("I shall not look
upon his like again," as Hamlet puts it.) The Christian ethic is replaced by an ethic of self-interested calculation administered by
men who would only "seem"—seem to be king, seem to be father,
seem to be deserving of our loyalty. (As *Othello*'s villainous Iago
proudly puts the same idea, as if what he was describing were a
new job skill that future employers would pay a lot for, "I am not
what I am.") To his credit, Hamlet knows not "seems": "I have that
within which passes show." He will instead perform his grief, his
sense of grievance, and his unhappiness. He will stage his resentment for this new life under an uncle who merely plays at being
the father. Unhappily, as Hamlet is soon to discover, the future is
owned by these men—Claudius, Fortinbras—who are good at

seeming but who are in truth "rank and gross in nature." They'll wear their heart on their sleeves "for daws to peck at," as Iago says, but then go on about their murderous business.

Because he sees the hypocrites for what they are from the beginning, Hamlet understands all that Othello misses, although he is not capable of doing much with his knowledge. What is clear to Hamlet that is obscure to Othello is that any kindness on his part will be answered only with cruelty. Thus his despair: to defeat my enemy I must become like him and thus most unlike my father. A large part of Hamlet's tragedy is that he has no choice but to enter the Machiavellian realm of realpolitik in which honesty is bad strategy. And so in spite of himself and in spite of his first protest in the play that he "knows not seeming," he falls immediately into "seeming" to be mad (although given his quandary a little real madness was in order). Hamlet is not pleased with himself because of the cleverness of his ploy. Rather, his dissembling fills him with self-loathing. More maddening still: Hamlet understands that he has little choice in his tactics because his enemy's cruelty can easily cloak itself in the mantle of virtue. In the absence of real justice, virtue is what the king says it is. And so in order to confront the Machiavellian hypocrites, Hamlet must become one of them and in the process feel viscerally that he is conspiring against himself. He has become his own enemy.

I think Hamlet's predicament is in most ways our own. We have no access to virtue because it is owned by pitiless hypocrites. Worse yet, we also feel that for some inescapable reason our efforts to confront the hypocrites have made us like them. We cannot confront them without feeling like we're conspiring against ourselves. This is grim stuff, I confess, but let me try a "what if." What if our primary moral conviction were not the Golden Rule, "Love thy neighbor as thyself," or "Do unto others as you would have them do unto you"? What if the passing of the father and his ethic meant not that there was no recourse to ethics but that another ethic was in order? I ask this not because I think there's something wrong with the Golden Rule as a rule—what Immanuel Kant called a "moral maxim," as something to be universalized in a community—but because it seems to me unavailable to us in the present, just as Hamlet found it unavailable in his own. (This is perhaps one of the many reasons that the Danish prince still seems to us so modern.)

The problem in the present is that even if we wanted to use the Rule and to know it (which is to say, to *live* it), we wouldn't know how. This is so for many reasons. We are prevented from living the Golden Rule by hypocrisy, by isolation from others, by our servility to established social orders, by our willingness to conspire in our own defeat, and, last and most inglorious, we are defeated by that matrix of moral failure combining hypocrisy, isolation, servility, and self-defeat, our own apocalyptic beast: the Holy Whore.

I will take these obstacles to contemporary ethical life up one at a time before returning to this fanciful "what if" concerning an alternative ethic.

Hypocrisy

We are mostly hypocrites in relation to our professed Christian ethic, the Golden Rule. That is, we imagine that we live it without actually living it. We believe that we operate by the Golden Rule while authorizing the use of the most abominable violence against others through B-52s, Black Hawk helicopters, Stinger missiles, and the rest of our dreaded arsenal. We routinely employ this arsenal in the ordinary pursuit of political and economic well-being, as if there was nothing the world needed more than a good bombing now and then, stubborn as it is to see that we represent its own best interests. Terrorists in Pakistan? Find them and bomb them. If a dozen women and children get in the way, that's "incidental." No need even for a lukewarm apology. Suffer the children to come to me? In our actions we say, "Sometimes the children will have to suffer." It's all for the "greater good," of course. When we claim, in such a world-political context, to "love our neighbors as ourselves," we become like the "hypocrites and scribes" censored by Jesus. We become mere advocates to the letter and not the substance of the Moral Law. As John Ruskin wrote, "I know no previous instance in history of a nation's establishing a systematic disobedience to the first principles of its professed religion" (*Unto this Last*, 57).

To put this in terms made famous by Immanuel Kant, evil is the act through which we place desire before duty. Claudius, for instance, put desire for power, fame, and the bed of his brother's wife, well before duty to his brother-the-king. This evil becomes a "radical evil" when it is institutionalized. Once evil is institutionalized, it becomes not simply something bad or self-serving that someone does; it becomes something that one is *born into*. Hitler was evil, but Nazi Germany was radically evil because it made evil the context of the world into which future generations of Germans would be born. For ourselves, twenty-first-century North Americans, the federal government's institutionalizing of a morality of desire becomes clearer with each passing administration. The duty to serve the public good always takes second place to the desire to preserve class interest. For instance, the preservation of a healthy environment for citizens is a civic duty for elected officials, but this duty is always trumped by the need to preserve wealth and structures of political and corporate power. It's not that Dick Cheney wants to despoil the wilderness or cause global warming; he's simply got other priorities. And certainly if there was ever a president willing to act on his own desire (to gain access to oil, to enrich his associates, to revenge his father against Saddam Hussein), it is our own G. W. Bush. To be sure, he feels obliged to cloak his self-interested actions in the mantle of "duty." He claims that it is his first duty as president to protect citizens. He opposes evil. He protects innocents. He seeks to extend freedom. Of course, it is equally plausible and more demonstrable that he extends evil, kills innocents, and imposes dominion. If I am right to say that his actions are a reflection of desire and his apologies a mere hypocritical gesture to duty, then the only maxim that his foreign policy projects is simply this: "It is ethical to enrich oneself at the expense of others." It is the perception of this latent "ethic" that prompts Europeans and Middle Easterners to resent us and call us hypocrites (we are "infidels"— unfaithful to what we should know to be the truth, even our own Christian truths).

Contrary to what the fundamentalist Christians among us imagine, evil in our world is not the irrational business of a fantastic "beast," a Satan, nor is it the breaking of a Commandment. The "horror," as Joseph Conrad's Mr. Kurtz put it, is the fraudulence of a system that claims to be moral while betraying morality. In Conrad's *Heart of Darkness*, the "noble cause of Progress" is nothing other than grubbing after coin. Europe is a "whited sepulcher," or death painted over.[1] The macabre work of the Company, in Gravesend, England, was the true heart of darkness. The heart of darkness is not at the end of the Congo River winding into the tenebrous African dark in a place of rendezvous with the devilish Mr. Kurtz; the true heart of darkness was where the tale *began*: behind a handsome walnut door in a corporate office not much different from the corporate offices of our day, just beyond a desk where two secretaries stood watch, "knitting black wool." It was from this removed place that European colonialism asked, Who are we? Who are they? What do we want? What legitimates our actions? Colonialism answered—violently—all these fundamental human questions through its actions. What Conrad saw in African colonialism during his famous trip into King Leopold's Belgian Congo, and what he depicted in *Heart of Darkness*, was the most grotesque and debasing hypocrisy. As he wrote, "The conquest of the earth, which mostly means the taking it away from those who have a different complexion or slightly flatter noses than ourselves, is not a pretty thing when you look into it too much" (50). Conrad called it the "merry dance of death and trade," an apt description to this day. The Gulf Wars are the dance of death and trade overlaid with the most transparently false claims to serving the universal good. When war profiteers have the political authority to decide when to make war and cloak their self-interested decision in claims to "justice," bowing their heads at church on Sunday just long enough for the cameras from the Associated Press to catch the image, that is hypocrisy. The piles of the unrequited dead make it difficult not to say that it is also evil. Just as with Jesus's antagonism with the Pharisees, official interpreters of the Jewish Law within the Roman state-sanctioned temple, the source of radical evil is not extraworldly. It is "statutory."

Because this evil is "radical" and no one individual's personal failing, it is not effective to try to elect honest people to take the place of the dishonest. Because if these honest people are smart (and we should hope that they are, I suppose), the first thing they will learn is that their honesty is their own worst enemy. They will learn that to be successful they must mask their honesty, wear their heart on their sleeves for Washington's pigeons to peck at, and come at their objectives in a way that is compromised from the first. We might hope that these methods will in the long run be in the name of the public good, but we should recognize that the acceptance of these less than fully honest methods is already a little defeat. In this way we aid and abet those we call enemy.

As Paul Ricoeur puts it, "Worse than injustice is one's own justice" (*The Conflict of Interpretations*, 438). *In our culture, malicious intent asks us to acknowledge as virtuous what is in reality virtue's betrayal.* The most unequivocal way to put this is to say that we are not a Christian culture. We have a majority Christian heritage in which we may now and then find troubling ruins of a promised ethic, but we have on the whole so thoroughly and so long ago forgotten Christianity's core teachings that it is as if they never really existed. And so the religion based on St. Paul's admonition to "abandon your wealth and give it to the poor" as a precondition of membership in the community of Jesus has become "your personal wealth is a reflection of God's blessings on you for having the good sense to be a Republican as well as a Christian." If God loves you in evangelical America, he will shower you with coin! The Christian "wager" (in Blaise Pascal's phrase) is now a kind of long-term investment strategy.

But there are other ways of looking at the situation, and they are not so abstruse, although they are certainly not familiar to the reign of the evangelical right. As Ricoeur points out in his superb study *Figuring the Sacred*, Christian ethics is in part the Judaic morality of equivalence ("do unto others" is an extension and an inversion of "an eye for an eye") and in part the novel morality of "superabundance." Christianity urges us to love not only our neighbor (an easy thing, especially when he loves you back) but our enemy as well. Give without expecting a return. This is a morality of *nonequivalence*. But when you give without the expectation of receiving an equivalent, you will receive "a good measure, pressed down, shaken together, running over" that will be "put into your lap" (Luke 6:38).

Are we a culture of equivalence? When it is in our interest, especially when the vengeance of an "eye for an eye" seems useful, we are. Are we a culture of Christian nonequivalence understood as the presumption of common abundance? Individually, certainly, we all are at times. We can be individually generous without expectation of return. But on the whole, as a culture, the assumption is that our well-being is dependent on capitalism, not Christianity. Rather than thriving in the certainty of a common abundance, we prefer to "prosper" through a competition that seeks necessarily to find those populations (whether slaves, the poor, women, working people, or, most recently, distant third world people) from whom value in the form of profit may be wrung. As John Kenneth Galbraith put it, speaking of American affluence in the 1950s (when in fact there was a good deal *more* income equality than there is at present), we are already this society of abundance that the Bible speaks of, but it is not a common abundance. Rather, our abundance is the spectacle of "private opulence and public squalor." In fact, our abundance is an opulence that believes it cannot exist without squalor. Put another way, what does your credit card company tell you about our culture's ethics? Jesus said, "Lend, expecting nothing in return" (Luke 6:29–30). Yet banks do legally what is forbidden to the Mafia: loan sharking. Personal bankruptcy was up 400 percent in the 1990s during one of the most prosperous decades in U.S. history. In the early years of the following Bush administration, credit card interest rates were at 18 to 19 percent, while the prime rate was 1 percent! What does that say about who we are? And that's what we do to *ourselves*.[2]

Or, watching Fox Cable News, one is always hearing the distant echo of our Protestant fathers, like Richard Baxter: "If God show [*sic*] you a way in which you may lawfully get more than in another way . . . if you refuse this and choose the less gainful way, you cross one of the ends of your calling and you refuse to be God's steward . . . you may labor to be rich for God" (quoted in Weber, 110). In the Fox worldview, if you are poor it is because you have perversely refused to be rich. Worse yet, by being poor you have blasphemed against God.

This, of course, is not news. But in a time when our noses are habitually rubbed in the pious posturing of our political leaders who continue to maintain that there is no tension between the purposes of business and Jesus, it is worth remembering. Perhaps we should say of a Christian ethic what Gandhi said of Western democracy: "It would be a good idea." In the meanwhile, it is just as Nietzsche saw it. For the oligarchs, good is whatever they are. Good = aristocratic = beautiful = happy = loved by the Gods. Cheney, Rummy, Wolfy, Condi, and the rest of that neo-con pack are Nietzsche's "beast of prey, the blond brute."[3] But this culture of authority is not limited to these rock stars, these icons of political strength. It penetrates to every level of authority from the corporate boardroom to the petty province of the college administrator or city manager. This culture in the end feels itself under no moral obligation other than the exercise of its own strength. They enjoy the most intense of human privileges: not to have to take seriously for too long their own disasters and misdeeds. And, truth be told, I wouldn't begrudge them this privilege quite so much if they were upfront about it. Instead, they wrap themselves in a mantle of Christian virtue as if it were a cloak of invisibility, but then feign to be shocked and outraged when the rest of the world surrounds them, pointing fingers, and says, "Behold, the hypocrite!"

Isolation

It's also difficult to talk about an ethic based on our relationship to others because we hardly have any relations to others. Never mind Middle Easterners. We hardly have relations with ourselves. We have relations to phantoms that fly past us in automobiles, high overhead in airplanes, and as truly mystifying images on TV, computers, and movie screens. These phantoms are so indifferent to us that they can't even bother to haunt us properly. In fact, it would be a good thing, real progress, if they did haunt us a bit. "I saw a man driving in a red car today. He looked at me. Who was he?" We should be more bothered by these apparitions who are nothing less than the *other humans with whom we live*, although you could never tell that by the way we behave. In Christian terms, they ought to be our church. The church is where the people gather in shared conviction. We should not wonder, "Who are these other people and what is my relationship to them?"

"I saw a woman today at the market. She placed an almond on her tongue. Suddenly there was a bitterness in my mouth! Who was she?"

What can it mean to "do unto others" or have them "do unto us" when most of the people we know are like creatures living in a parallel dimension? You are aware of them, and maybe you can imagine talking to them, but it seems to you impossible and maybe a little ridiculous to try. Oh, every once in a while we're thrust together and obliged to speak, but more often than not it's as if we are rockfish and have just been introduced to a species of octopus. Our sense of others is a sort of alienation. They are mysterious to us and quickly threatening. The most extreme face of this experience is racism, but racism, bad as it is in itself, also serves to hide the alien feelings we have about *all* other humans, even those most like us. In their cars. With their shopping carts. Even our wives and children come to seem strange and inessential to us. In this culture, 50 percent of married couples "grow apart" into divorce. Even our families seem arbitrary and ephemeral, something we can trade in when "things just aren't working out" or "my needs aren't getting met."[4]

The true church in which we are human together has been lost. Instead, we have a false church in which our relations to each other are either statutory or hallucinatory. Consider Katie Couric. Larry King says she is America's sweetheart. Don't we know her, fantastical though she is, better than we know the people two doors down?

"I love Katie's smile. I feel like she's a member of my own family."

Our relationship to others is "hypermediated." That's a philosophical way of saying that there is always something between us that makes human *im*mediacy impossible. And not just something but layers of somethings in between. Home itself, our neighborhoods, have become not a way of being together but something between us. Listen to this, hearken to it, as the Bible encourages: "Home isolates."

Let that sink down.

Our homes isolate us from others as if those others were a sort of contamination. Isn't that the real social meaning of SARS, West Nile virus, and now avian flu? Other people are dangerous, especially (as ever!) those teeming Asians. The *outdoors* is dangerous, as our health departments remind us during mosquito season, so stay inside after dusk. Inside, where your TV is waiting up for you with its gray-blue light of comfort. In Boccaccio's *The Decameron*, ten wealthy and privileged young people of Florence flee to a villa in the countryside in order to wait out the pestilence of the Black Plague. They isolate themselves while blaming the dead for abandoning them. They make literal the hyperbolic idea that the dead should bury the dead. Or, as our hats and bumper stickers are now prepared to say, "Fuck everybody." There is an antihome within our homes where we go for the cold comfort provided by TV, telephones, iPods, and computers. This media (literally, that which comes between) isolates us, and at a certain level we believe it protects us from others.

For example, we have a lot to do with Iraqis these days, but how many of us know an Iraqi, have shaken hands with an Iraqi, have eaten with an Iraqi? We will spend millions of dollars each day for years to come on our relationship with the Iraqi people, and we will know none of them. It almost makes you long for the days when wars were between cousins and brothers. Greeks and Trojans. Athenians and Spartans. Pandavas and Dhartarashtras. Sunnis and Shiites. French (Franks, after all) and Germans. North against South. At least that devastation had a human and tragic dimension. At least you knew the people you killed. In the *Bhagavad Gita*, the pathos of Arjuna's situation before the great battle was that he lacked the moral will to rise in order to kill a cousin. That's how difficult any war ought to be. But here, we go from the false home of the TV and the computer screen, where the next generation of fighter pilots receives his first training, straight to the cockpit of the fighter jet where the enemy is so many blips on the screen.

For us in the present, it's like Orson Welles in the gondola of the Ferris wheel in *The Third Man*. Harry Lime rises high over Vienna and over the future. He indicates people moving below. "Would you really feel any pity if one of those dots stopped moving forever? If I offered you $20,000 for every dot that stops, would you really, old man, tell me to keep my money—or would you calculate how many dots you could afford to spare?" Only that distance represented by the height of the Ferris wheel allows a dehumanizing of those "dots" that makes it possible to think of them through an astringent economic rationality. The irony here, of course, is that Harry Lime was the supposed enemy of the victorious and morally acute Western Allies (that moral superiority is made tangible by Trevor Howard's brilliant performance as Colonel Calloway). But of course it was just exactly those Western countries that would work hardest in the postwar era to implement Lime's profitable ethic. It is Western, corporate, globalized capital that has worked to turn people into dots for the purpose of more efficiently working a complex economic apparatus. Move this many millions of people out of industry and into high tech. No, the high tech is going to India. So, move this many millions of people out of high tech and into the service sector. Not needed there? Well, then they're just not needed. Many millions of our fellow citizens are told in not subtle ways on a daily basis that they are basically not needed. For anything. Ever. It is with these people that we fill our ever-growing prison systems. Our prisons are a form of warehousing for people who have been told from their youngest age that an education would be wasted on them because they are not needed.

We're not even dots on the ground anymore. We're pixels on a computer screen. We're the balances in a cost/benefit analysis. We're the bytes in a data bank.

"How many dots, old boy?"

The great technical rationalizing forces in our world have forbidden all alternative understandings of our world, including an authentic Christian understanding. As a consequence, we have lost all capacity for understanding the world as ethical except in the statutory and fraudulent terms of the false church of the corporate state. Just as important, we have lost all sense of the world as sacred, as a reality deserving of reverence. Instead, we have a sense of infinite complicity, a sense of being integrated, whether we like it or not, into what is not good. This complicity has become so normalized that we hardly recognize it as the source of our sense of guilt and even keen despair. Is there anything that feels more "normal" to us than our jobs? And yet the human relations found there are mostly about what the Italian philosopher Antonio Negri calls "the sociality of money." Our human relations are first and foremost about relations of money. If you have a colleague at work, is your relationship with him or her about a primary interest in that person or about the fact that you are both being paid to be in this one place for eight (and increasingly more than eight) hours a day? Wouldn't you say about this person, in your heart of hearts, "Only the arbitrariness of this job thrusts us together. I would never choose to be with this person because I have nothing in common with him"? It's like the earlier mentioned octopus next to a rockfish. They both slink around the same reefs and the same kelp beds each day, but the one is always seeing the other as foreign, strange, and a little bit scary. "What's it like in his head?" we are forever wondering about those closest to us.

I often ask my students, "Why are you here? Why am I here? What's our relationship?" Most of my students attend college because they think it will lead to a better job, which really only means more money, which really only means more stuff for them. This is the result of no stupidity or corruption on their part. They can see perfectly what's what in the culture. For them it is simply a question of surviving in a social and economic order that was well established long before they were born. If that order is evil, it is not an evil that they feel responsible for. Anything like real thought is not useful to the purpose of survival in such a system. They'll worry about questions of complicity, of something called the "sociality of money" later, if ever (oh, they may also hope that the concept isn't on the final exam because they really didn't get it). Mostly, they just want to get away from people like me who will ask them to think about such questions as "Am I complicit in an order that is evil?" In this way, they are perfectly like the world they grow up into. But it's difficult to blame them for that.

Servility

We have no sense of having chosen this social evil even though we reconfirm it daily simply by getting up and living it. This situation is nothing that any of us would sit down and choose either individually or as a group. Rather, we feel bound to it. We are captive to systems and assumptions that produce these effects. *We are free, but our will is servile.* How many of us, when we pay our federal taxes, feel as if we are collaborators in activities and purposes we could never justify? How many of us even bother to wonder just what it is that is done with our tax dollars? Our money to the military, to war profiteers, to a wasteful, toxic, and cruel food industry, to internationalizing economic exploitation, to the pillaging of the natural world, to the endless asphalting of the country.[5] Our money to provide for the needs of the automobile (hundred of billions of dollars each year for the construction and repair of highways), our lives organized according to the needs of machines. Here's a simple question: Whose needs do we more adequately provide for? The needs of the car or the needs of children threatened by hunger, sickness, and illiteracy?

In an editorial, Bob Herbert wrote that "the State of Florida really knows how to hurt a kid."

> It has money for sports stadiums. It lavishes billions of dollars' worth of tax breaks and other goodies on private corporations. It even has money for a substantial reserve fund. But, in

an episode of embarrassing and unnecessary tightfistedness, it has frozen enrollment in a badly needed state health insurance program for low-income children.

Florida is one of 34 states that have made serious cuts in public health insurance programs for low-income people over the past two years. A study by the Center on Budget and Policy Priorities found that from 1.2 million to 1.6 million men, women and children have lost coverage as a result.[6]

The paving of America proceeds apace at the rate of a Delaware of asphalt every year. Tax money is always available for that. Money for sick children is another matter. Of course, Governor Jeb Bush is "concerned," but, as Herbert reports, the governor feels that "this is a problem that requires a long-term, sustainable solution." In other words, don't expect anything to happen soon or ever.

Of course, the automobile is just one of the many things in this culture that are more important than the health of poor people and their children. Nonetheless, every time I get in my car, I do so with a sort of sigh, knowing that I am cooperating with a social order that is not only destructive but also self-destructive. And yet I do get in my car.

Our will is servile.

Under less oppressive circumstances, we would not choose these things, I believe, and yet we are captive to them. What choice do we have? Not pay taxes? Not work? Walk or ride bikes in the brutal Los Angelizing of our cities and towns both large and small? Here in Bloomington-Normal, Illinois, we have a beltway that circles the city called Veterans' Parkway. It is six lanes and a massive median with strip malls and auto dealerships on all sides. ("Sounds like home!" you say.) Virtually no provision was made for anyone to walk along it and certainly not to cross it. And yet some do. Recently, I've begun to pay more attention to those who walk our parkway. They are children. They are old. They are poor. They are, increasingly, Mexican migrant workers and their families. They scramble across the six lanes, trying to get to supermarkets and megastores, with about as much provision for their safety as crossing an interstate. For most of its length, it is *illegal* to cross this parkway on foot. There are no crosswalks or walk signals, so if you want to cross it on foot you must jaywalk. The people who do cross on foot have more in common with crushed raccoons than they have with those of us all properly seat-belted in our cars. To me, this scene is a symbol for what our culture is at present. This symbol needs to be read. It needs to be the pretext for thought. It needs to be understood. It cannot be merely the occasion for a remark along the lines of "What's that fool doing running across the street? He's going to get killed!"

Phantoms.

We are captive to a world of phantoms, and we are captive to do what is not good. We experience evil as a kind of reign, as if we were Jews under the Babylonian Captivity. We're in exile. But from what?

As a teacher, the older I get, the clearer it is to me that I'm in the classroom because I'm getting paid to be there. I am a teacher, and yet I am also clearly part of the way in which our culture has been totalized by money. The need to find a place within the system of money is inescapable. One of the things that I always say to my most serious writing students is that regardless of the strength of their commitment to writing, and regardless of their individual talent, in order to live in this culture they will always also have to find a way to interrupt the flow of money. Money is liquid. It flows. You will have to find a way to make it flow through you and your bank account. That means you will have to sit in one of money's circuits. Apart from inherited wealth, that inevitably means a J-O-B.[7]

So, as the son of a very much lower-middle-class American family, I too have had to find a place where I can interrupt the flow of money. For me, teaching has been a way to provide for the greater freedom of being a writer. Granted, being a professor is close to what Stanley Aronowitz calls the "last good job," because unlike virtually any other job, it structures time for entirely self-directed creativity (or, as it is called institutionally, "research"). Of course, "research" is a much-contested notion in state legislatures at appropriation time. Like the seven-year return of cicadas, professors are periodically the object of legislative inquisitions about the value of their "research productivity," with the unspoken assumption that all this research is just a screen for laziness and unaccountability. The result of such legislative studies always reveal that in fact professors work fifty to sixty hours per week. That never convinces the Board of Higher Education of anything more than the certainty that they're getting scammed, so they'll keep doing studies until they find one that tells them what they want it to tell them. Faculty research activities should have a "tangible, measurable benefit to the people of the state of Illinois" (so said James Kaplan, chairman of the Illinois Board of Higher Education). The stink of economic rationalism is not far from this demand for the "measurable." The implied threat is that if the activities of professors are found to be "wasteful," the board will work "rationally" in order to make it "productive." Productivity, from this perspective, of course only means the accumulation of wealth. So, professors are routinely asked, how do you provide for the material well-being of the people? They can't argue for spiritual well-being because in the legislature's neat logic, that is somebody else's business (the clergy).

But I think that education's social function is about spirit, or *should* be. Think about the damage that the Illinois Board of Higher Education's logic (understood as what Max Weber called the "spirit of capitalism") does to what I'd like to call the counterspirit of human demand. From the legislature's perspective, the bottom line (so to speak) is also a demand: "All work should be measurable. Creativity is a luxury or something for leisure time." This thinking is entirely the result of economic rationalism driven by notions rising out of the merger of the Protestant ethic and capitalism: efficiency, asceticism, and profit. We are abjectly servile to this logic as a culture. But why, we might ask, shouldn't legislators as representatives of the people argue in the name of a counterdemand to the business community? Why shouldn't they say, "All people should have the opportunity for the creativity that professors enjoy." If all workers had "research" opportunities, time for their own private inventive interests, perhaps the gulf between the academy and the community would disappear. Instead of this, we get an insistence on shared misery. Even other workers share in this insistence and roundly resent the idea of professors and their supposedly light workloads. *Everyone* should share equally in oppression, in the diminishing of human creativity, or so they would seem to argue. This is the weird form that the Golden Rule takes among much of the middle and lower-middle classes in the present: *"Have done to others what has been done to you."*

I guess misery really does love company.

I was lucky enough to grow up in a time when the culture thought it might need more smart people than the upper classes could provide on their own. The state university systems exploded in the 1960s as a result of the country's anxiety about what the Soviet Union was doing in space and elsewhere. So people like me were able to take advantage of the moment and claim degrees (cultural capital) that had never before been available to us. When I finished high school, I was told, "It's time to go to college." Twenty years earlier there would have been no necessary reason that a person from my social class would finish high school, never mind college.

In the aftermath of the Cold War, the need for higher education is being reconsidered. Enormous state educational systems are essentially bankrupt. In many cases, it's simply a sort of inertia that carries them forward. Tuition soars, class size grows, tenure is under assault, and non–tenure track teachers are a large and growing percentage of the workforce, turning many disciplines into "fields" for migratory workers with Ph.D.s on whose resentful backs budgets are balanced. Still, legislators continue to complain about education's lack of material usefulness and the university's failure to be economically rational. But you never hear this sort of talk in the country's elite private institutions. Intelligence, knowledge, and creativity are perquisites of the wealthy, and their institutions will continue to foster all three. It is only state universities, the people's universities, in theory, that have the burden of measuring every activity economically.

One of the old maxims of capitalism is that "money always returns to its rightful owners" (i.e., to the hereditary wealthy). In much the same way, we might argue that cultural capital always returns to its rightful owners. In the post–Cold War era, intelligence, knowledge, and creativity can now safely return to the privileged classes who can send their children to prep schools and Ivy League colleges. The rest of us can go to the equivalent of vocational schools, or we can become "trash," the steadily growing class of the not-needed.

It's sad if you think about this state of affairs, but it's even sadder if you don't. But sad or not, we never seem to be shaken from our willingness to participate in what is clearly not a good system. Whether professor, or student, or office worker like Peter in *Office Space*, in the end we all collaborate. Our will is servile.

Conspiring in Our Own Defeat

Oddly, the institutional nature of evil, its presence among us as the most ordinary things like our jobs, taxes, the work of our military, cities organized around the needs of machines, leaves us oddly unaware of any personal responsibility. At best, we tend to wonder along with the Psalms, "For how long will the evil prosper and the virtuous suffer?" Isn't that essentially the question we ask when we see people like Dick Cheney thrive? But there is a problem with this perception because we seem not to know why we should take this evil upon ourselves. We don't sufficiently recognize our own participation in evil, or, to put it another way, our participation in our own defeat. Which means that the traditional Christian movement of sin, the consciousness of sin in guilt, and the confession of sin in redemption is not possible. I might even go so far as to say that it is structurally forbidden. Or forbidden as a matter of routine. Evil is routinized. Just as security forces routinize torture—"It's Wednesday, so today is the day I torture the radical Islamists"—so we work for two hours on Tuesday to support through our taxes the work of the projects of our own state terrorists. We don't know how to take responsibility for social and institutional evil, the Order of Law, onto ourselves. But it is critical that we learn how to take this evil upon ourselves because without doing so there is no possibility for reclaiming freedom from servility, no reason for hope, and no opportunity for the arrival of what Christianity calls the Kingdom of God, that place where everything may begin again.

The failure of the Golden Rule is not entirely explained by the hypocrisy of our leaders, nor by our individual isolation at "home," nor by the idea that we are captive to evil structurally through our jobs. We also participate in the delusion that the violence and the cruelty that is visited upon others in our name is in some way operating in our self-interest. *We will evil's continuance because we think it's good for us.* Beyond a political and economic system of evil, and beyond our structural complicity, there is a complicity of individual will. We are willing participants in evil, in spite of the fact that we imagine ourselves as good. Somewhere in that ocean of acute perception that we now know as *In Search of Lost Time* (1927), Marcel Proust makes the following observation. He says that the most common thing about humans is not common sense but human kindness. Unhappily, he goes on, our natural disposition to kindness is always defeated by self-interest.

This is something that has been observed time and again about Americans. We're a nice people, a generous people, a *kind* people. And yet the policies of our government are cruel and nakedly self-interested. In 1976, I was teaching composition at the University of Iowa when an exiled member of the administration of Salvador Allende asked whether he could speak to my class about what had happened in Chile with the CIA-sponsored overthrow of Allende's government and the murder of thousands of students and leftists. He said to my class, "You know, traveling in your country, a person cannot help but be impressed by your kindness. But you do not understand how cruel your government is. You do not understand what you do to the rest of the world when you elect these 'representatives.'"

Or, the obvious example of the moment: we have nothing against Muslims in the abstract. We have no reason to be unkind to them. But since they happen to be sitting on a huge proportion of the world's oil resources, we feel obliged to choose death *and worse* for them routinely. Our desire to be kind is routinely overwhelmed by our government's desire to act in what it perceives to be the self-interest (the gravely intoned "national interest") of the people it represents. Our kindness ends up expressed as violence.

Proust himself was always generous, or *kind*, before all else. But his native generosity became the acid of social criticism when his unflinching, unapologetic regard fell on the cruelty of self-interest. He considered cruelty more than anything else just maddeningly, puzzlingly, infinitely *stupid*. The stupidity of class arrogance. The stupidity of anti-Semitism. The stupidity of homophobia. Time and again, he discovered the self-interested desire to be an aristocrat, to have wealth, or simply to get laid at the root of the most unspeakable cruelty. For the infinitely gentle Marcel Proust, deliberate unkindness, especially when motivated by self-interest, hurt him and angered him more than anything else he could name.

But I think we need to add something to Proust's observation. We need to add the further irony that we are wrong to think that cruelty functions in our self-interest. Cruelty does not work. In both the short and long run, cruel efforts to maintain self-interest have the consequence of *making us conspire against ourselves*. By acting cruelly in our self-interest, we actually become conspirators in our own defeat.

You might call this the law of political karmic return. The CIA calls it blowback and figures it into the cost of doing business. I think it is more insidious than that. We conspire against ourselves in all sorts of ways, most of which are so familiar that they seem almost like common sense. The root problem is that all of our decisions go into a rational machinery, a social calculus of "benefit." Thus, the infamous "cost/benefit analysis." This is not solely the logic of corporations. The corporations depend on the fact that it will also be the logic of consumers! So, the Wal-Mart company assumes that people will shop at its stores because they will perceive that by shopping there they get an "added value." They get lower prices. They can buy more things with the same dollars. The people themselves believe that by shopping at Wal-Mart, they receive a "surplus." They believe that they receive more than they have paid for.

Of course, the hidden cost is this: Wal-Mart can keep its costs low by keeping its wages low (its labor cost), by denying unions, and by exporting the manufacturing of the things it sells to places, most notoriously China, where the wages are even lower. Worse yet, Wal-Mart's competitors are then forced to adopt the same tactics in order to compete with Wal-Mart's strategy. Recognizing that low wages, lack of worker protection, lack of benefits like health care, exportation of jobs, rising unemployment and deskilling of the workforce are part of the true cost of this business is the beginning of an alternative way of thinking about value. The true cost that follows in short order is simply poverty and all of its attendant negatives (damage to mental and physical health, to family stability, and to education).

Shoppers at Wal-Mart undermine their own interests. They participate willingly (if with servility) in an economic order that is nothing short of cruel in its ultimate consequences, and it is cruelest of all, paradoxically, for many of those who consider Wal-Mart their "family" store. Of course, it's well known now, following the recent successful litigation against Wal-Mart's employment practices, that Wal-Mart gives a new monstrous dimension to the idea of the dysfunctional family. Because it has systematically obliged its employees to work off the clock, it has created within its family a sort of part-time slavery. "You will work for poverty wages with inadequate health and retirement benefits and beyond that you will work for X hours per week for nothing." (To add insult to injury, it has been revealed in class action lawsuits against the company that some of this off-the-clock work was during what were supposed to be lunch breaks. So, not only were the workers coerced into working for nothing, but they had to do it with low blood sugar!)[8]

We used to call people who worked for nothing slaves. Not anymore. Slavery is creative business planning. Part-time slavery is the centerpiece of Wal-Mart's strategic plan. Wal-Mart has even outdone the fantastic scheme of Nikolai Gogol's character Chichikov in *Dead Souls* (1842). Chichikov bought the legal title to dead peasants in order to seem to be the aristocratic owner of thousands of serfs. Wal-Mart has its own "dead-peasant policy": it takes out life insurance on its employees and names itself as their sole beneficiaries. Unlike the foolish Chichikov, Wal-Mart makes sure that its corporate-owned life insurance makes a neat actuarially driven profit off of the dead. So in the American economy of the future, you will work for the company not only off the clock but after you are dead! Now that's American entrepreneurial genius at its best!

Most unhappily, where Wal-Mart goes, others must follow in order, as they explain, to "stay competitive." In an article by Steven Greenhouse, it was revealed that all across the country workers are being forced to work off the clock for corporations.

> In interviews and in affidavits supporting employee lawsuits, Ms. LeBlue and more than 50 workers from a dozen companies said they were required to do such unpaid work despite federal and state laws that prohibit it and despite recent lawsuits against Wal-Mart and other companies that have highlighted the problem.[9]

These companies include A&P, JPMorgan Chase, Pep Boys, Ryan's Family Steakhouses, TGF Precision HairCutters, SmartStyle, Radio Shack, and Starbucks.

To take self-interest as self-defeat to another level, those more affluent among us, the owners of what Marx called the "means of production," can reason, "If I clear-cut this forest, I can sell the timber and plant soybeans for export to China, a very profitable move. But if I cut down the forest, we may not have air to breathe or a stable climate in the future. Animals will be deprived of habitat. Species may go extinct. Oh, fuck it, why should my forest be responsible for the future when it can be profitable now?"

This is not the exclusive logic of corporate capitalists, although it was certainly the logic of factory trawlers when they stripped the Atlantic of cod from Nova Scotia to the Chesapeake, a grave crime against the cod (but who the hell ever thinks about what the ugly-mug cod need?), humanity, and the future.[10] This is also the logic of Brazil's left-wing government led by Luiz Inácio Lula da Silva. Brazil's deforestation of the Amazon increased by 40 percent in 2003 alone. To be sure, President da Silva's rationale involved the importance of a cash crop to feed the urban poor. "The Amazon is not untouchable," said da Silva.[11] This, obviously, places the burden of feeding the poor squarely on the backs of parrots and leopards.

Meanwhile, Brazilian agribusiness kings like Blairo Maggi make conflict of interest a virtual requirement for governance. Not only is Maggi owner of one of the largest soybean production and export companies in Brazil; he is also the governor of the state of Mato Grasso ("dense jungle"). Thanks to the "prosperity" he brings, the Amazon will soon be just another fantastical postmodern location, so familiar to North Americans, where the names of places no longer have any relationship to what's actually in the place. Mato Grasso will refer to a place that is no more than a factory for exchange value in a soybean monoculture, just as Illinois is a "prairie state" with 0.1 percent of its original prairie remaining. Of course, once the original plant/animal/human inhabitants are gone, we wax sentimental. The things we slaughter become our heritage. We wear feathers in our hair and go to summer powwows.

The jungle or the prairie, parrots or bobolinks—none of them ever have the opportunity to argue their own value as *being*, things that deserve respect simply because they are. This reveals a grave spiritual flaw in their masters—the governors, developers, and agribusiness kings of the world. The ruling order has no moral right to rule because it makes its multiform daily purpose the defeat of the future. The logic that concludes that our "interest" is about "profit" assures a future defined by cruelty (usually rationalized as "collateral damage" or "incidental take"), but in the long run, it will be understood as self-defeat. (No big deal. That's why CNN and the Weather Channel specialize in disaster. When our own defeat comes, we'll be able to redeem it as something "interesting" and "entertaining." Fun for the whole miserable family.)

Self-interest is indistinguishable from local and global legalized violence (all accomplished with the blessing of the morality of "market freedom") aimed at humans, the natural world, and ultimately being itself, before which our captains of state stand with all the wonder of a gourmand before a steak. They're going to eat it up. What if our kindness-defeating self-interest is only, from the perspective of the future, the repeated application of a rapacious and self-defeating logic?

As essayist James Howard Kunstler puts it pointedly, "We've sunk so much of our national wealth into a particular way of doing things that we're psychologically compelled to defend it even if it drives us crazy and kills us."[12]

Chapter 3

Confessions of a Holy Whore

1.

It is no doubt the case that at some level we believe that these things that separate us from the Golden Rule have a payoff: they allow the accumulation of wealth while making the idea that we're responsible for others not so much wrong as irrelevant. And so it's all right if 60 percent of the nation's wealth is owned by the top 4 percent of the population. And apparently it's all right if very little of that wealth is spread about as generosity, or caring, or even as a tax write-off for charity. As the Newtithing Group (a philanthropic research organization) reported in December 2005, the least generous of all working-age Americans are those who make in excess of $10 million annually. This group had on average $101 million in investment assets and made charitable gifts equal to 1.5 percent of their assets. So what's trickling where? Ask Richard Grasso, former head of the New York Stock Exchange, who left his job with a multimillion-dollar payout. Greed begets more greed. Nothing ever really trickles down except suffering, and suffering can trickle a very long way. (That's globalization!) The idea that capitalism ultimately works in everyone's interest is but one in capitalism's extensive repertoire of scams. Like an original sin, this assumption is capitalism's original con. Worse yet, we have bought into this malign logic in spite of its real and visible results. This, again, is the condition that Kant described as "radical evil": even though we wish individually to be people of goodwill, because we lack ethical principles to unite us, we behave as if we were "instruments of evil."

But the difficulty of our situation is even more complex than the mistaken assumptions about our self-interest can explain. Imagine that we were to try to find a place entirely outside complicity, completely uncontaminated by the logic of self-interest, from which point we could attack the plutocratic assumptions of the present with political purity. In short, what would happen if we tried to rise above self-interest in order to return to the sacred? If the "system" is evil, what options do we have for standing *outside* the system in freedom rather than servility?

Hamlet, again, is the emblem of this dilemma. Hamlet's gloominess is the consequence not simply of his adolescence but of the fact that he sees too clearly that in order to restore goodness to the world he will have to become his own enemy and thus make himself a hypocrite, isolate himself from his family and community, become a public menace to those he loves (especially poor Ophelia), and ultimately participate in his own defeat. If his efforts only lead to the ascendance of Fortinbras, he might as well have left old Claudius where he was—on his father's throne and between his mother's legs. Hamlet "can't win for losing," as the folk saying puts it. He can't win because every effort to win has the opposite effect. Hamlet understood, with a pertinence that is powerful to this day, that the only means available to him for confronting his enemy made his enemy stronger. Hamlet's dilemma is prototypical of what German filmmaker Rainer Werner Fassbinder called the Holy Whore.

The difficulty in finding a political "outside" innocent of complicity was a primary drama in Fassbinder's movies in the 1970s. He tried to make his art think between two brutal facts. On the one hand, there was Germany's postwar Economic Miracle, the rise of a tremendously profitable modern corporate capitalism. What Fassbinder saw more clearly than any other artist of his moment was how easily, how smoothly, how *happily* fascism survived in the new model of corporate capitalism. The film *The Marriage of Maria Braun* is really about the marriage of the ethics of fascism with the economic machinery of capitalism. For Fassbinder, capitalism had something very simple to teach fascism: don't kill those you consider inferior to you. Exploit them, and with a clear conscience since you *still don't believe they're human.* This logic certainly applies to Europe's increasingly angry Middle Eastern populations who have been exploited economically for decades, but it also applies to our own relation to Mexican maquiladoras and Asian sweatshops, including China's state-sanctioned sweatshops and prison factories. When we shop for cheap foreign-produced goods at our discount shopping stores, we know at some level that the people who created these goods are being exploited. We also know at an even deeper and morally murkier level that that's OK because these people are, after all, "little brown people" and they need the work, even if it is work that only maintains poverty. We are thus, just as Kant described, people of goodwill working as instruments of evil.[1]

Fassbinder never seriously considered the impatient and violent revolutionary politics of the Beider-Meinhoff gang as a legitimate response to corporate fascism. Rather, he tried to imagine a place outside both the authority of the state and the counterauthority of the revolution. His strategy early on, in his Godard-influenced gangster films like *Love Is Colder Than Death* (1969), was protopunk. He employed the politics of ugly. He seemed to argue, "If the world is ugly, my art will be uglier than ugly. Thus will I achieve a new beauty. If my every effort to live and find love produces only death, then I will be deader than death." He even extended the politics of ugly to his own body. As he said late in his life, "Grow ugly and work. . . . I want to be ugly on the cover of *Time*—it'll happen and I'm glad about it and I admit it when ugliness has finally reclaimed all beauty. That is luxury" (Katz, 5).

At other times, as in *Ali: Fear Eats the Soul* (1973), Fassbinder tried to imagine that Dostoevsky's "Holy Fool" could be a sort of hero of the in-between, neither bourgeois nor revolutionary. Ali the Holy Fool, a Moroccan immigrant laborer in postwar Germany, hangs onto simple truths and direct feelings, a kind of wisdom that stands opposed to the brutality of business self-interest and everyday oppression. The Holy Fool was, finally, a politics of optimism insofar as Fassbinder could imagine an "outside" to the oppression he was concerned with. The evil in *Fear Eats the Soul* was still the evil of an articulate residue of fascism, although here it is in alliance with the shadowy and malevolent background of employers of foreign labor. Ali stood outside that evil, even though his outside, deprived of Dostoevsky's mysticism, was the hopeless otherness of a mere victim.

Subsequently, Fassbinder's interest came to focus more and more exclusively on fascism's successor, corporate capitalism. Postwar capitalism didn't oppose its victims; it didn't line them up and murder them. It *absorbed* its enemies. As Fassbinder said in an interview with Renate Klett in 1978:

> In 1933 it was perfectly clear to the people who emigrated: all this was going to change, it'll have to change, it can't stay this way. That was clear to everybody. It was a fatalistic form of fascism, which only worked because of the widespread urge for self-destruction, whereas this new form—and you mustn't call it fascism; that would be a distortion—what we have now is actually much worse because it's settling in for the duration. It'll all look perfectly innocuous, people will think they're living in a free country, etc. To me the development that's taking place right now seems more depressing somehow, because you really can't do anything to fight it. All you can do is keep your eyes open, and if you do, you certainly see the craziest things, if you look real hard. (Fassbinder, 134–35)

Fassbinder saw the importance of his own work not in terms of a social criticism of a fascist or authoritarian state but in terms of formal strategies for creating and maintaining an "outside." For the purposes of the argument I am trying to make, the notion of an outside is critical because it is through a viable outside, a sort of counterspirit to the spirit of capitalism, that the spirit of servility, our captivity to evil, can be effectively challenged. In his own moment, Fassbinder was certain that the outside was disappearing, and there didn't seem to be anything that even the most fearless and conscious adversary to the "inside" could do about it. The new ruling order didn't forbid art, no matter how adversarial that art tried to be; it simply digested or internalized it. It made its opposition captive to its own purposes. In his essay on Hanna Schygulla, "Not a Star, Just a Vulnerable Human Being Like the Rest of Us," Fassbinder wrote that he tried to maintain the authenticity of his artistic relationship with his "star," Schygulla, in spite of "the more or less successful attempts of an officious world to turn us into easily manipulated ciphers or marketable goods" (199).

Fassbinder did not fear murder or incarceration (although because of his acquaintance with Red Army Faction leader Andreas Baader that was not out of the question); he feared discovering himself dissolved by a system from which there was no exit. At the conclusion of Fassbinder's *The Merchant of Four Seasons* (1971), the lead character, the fruit peddler Hans Epp, deliberately drinks himself to death rather than continue to enjoy the material success of his fruit business. Here are his parting words to his best friend, his war buddy Harry:

HANS: Harry, you're the only real human being, but you're a swine, too.

HARRY: Sure. We're all swine.

HANS: That's right. But you're nothing more than a swine, a tiny, little swine.

This splendid illogic is at the heart of Fassbinder's new critique of what was in "for the duration." Even he who would remain human is one of the swine, and a "tiny, little" swine at that. Needless to say, conservatives hated the argument, but sixties-style German revolutionaries were not much happier. It did not describe a "correct line of analysis." In his criticism of the German revolutionary left, Fassbinder showed that by opposing the authority of the state with the authority of revolution, authority cannot lose. Similarly, one does not overthrow the Hollywood star system by being a movie star. Unfortunately, one has little choice about being or not being a movie star once one starts making movies. That decision is made elsewhere.

Fassbinder's more self-critical gesture beyond the holy fool was what he called the "Holy Whore." *Beware of a Holy Whore* (1970) is a veiled self-criticism of Fassbinder's work with the antitheater group in which he first worked and out of which he grew to international stardom. In the film, a group of actors is waiting in a Spanish villa, the gorgeous repose of the Mediterranean in the background, for the arrival of the Artist, the director (and Fassbinder double) Jeff. Jeff and his group exhibit two things: the unexamined habit of thinking of themselves as revolutionaries (the movie they make is a vague and always incomplete statement about "state brutality") and a formless sexual desire that metamorphoses easily into an irritable sadism. The characters brutalize each other not because brutality is the logical consequence of a philosophical or political thought. No one is even conscious that their brutal behavior is brutal. They brutalize each other out of an irritation that they can't seem to realize the transcendental pleasure their revolutionary assumptions have promised them. Where is the happiness of the revolutionary, he who is free and pure of the state?

In short, if they wanted to make a film about brutality, they ought to have made it about themselves first. Which is just what Fassbinder did. The only answer the actors find to this internal contradiction of the revolutionary is drinking *Cuba libres* and then smashing their glasses on the marble floors of the villa for the obliging (and brutalized) staff to clean up. (The fascist racism of *Ali* is the leftist racism of the German revolutionaries who behave with contempt for the dark-complexioned hotel staff.) The gesture is, of course, deluded ("We're like Ché because we drink *Cuba libres*"), and it is thoroughly complicit with the enemy because it is a drink made with capitalist Coca-Cola. Fassbinder's point couldn't be clearer.

The artists are both emotionally and financially dependent on the state. The film's thesis is delivered in an opening monologue by one of the actors who describes a Goofy cartoon in which Goofy mistakes a short crook (Wee Willy in cross-dress disguise) for a little girl. When the police at last capture Wee Willy and lead him away from an astonished Goofy, Goofy's only comment is "It must have been a shock for the poor little girl to find out she's a crook." Similarly, the holy warriors of the revolution must have been shocked to be told by Fassbinder that they were just whores to the state and its sadistic ethos. Even the revolution ends up being about oppression, as well as complicity, and self-destruction.

Oddly enough, this work of self-criticism did not lead to despair. The realization of complicity and self-defeat was not the end for Fassbinder. Rather, he had the cunning to see that an acknowledgment of complicity was the only honest and productive thing he could do. If artists have no choice but to be whores, they must make the acknowledgment of that complicity prominent. If the artist seeks to wear the mask of the holy, he must also point to the mask in order to indicate that it covers the face of a whore.

Differently put, as Stendahl wrote, art is the "promise of happiness." Taking up Stendahl's idea, Nietzsche wrote that this promise was the wish to "escape from torture." Art's dilemma is that this promise is never fulfilled and the torture is never completely escaped. This is so not because the world is tragic and bad but because art itself *is* the maintenance of the promise as *only a promise*, never seriously meant to be fulfilled. In the end, the artist is half in love with torture because it was exactly torture—the world as it stands—that made him an artist in the first place. However vivid art makes the combat between happiness and torture, it must live in a certain bad faith. It is not finally about the conquest of torture by the principle of happiness. Such happiness would require the death of art itself, and that is something the artist would find sadder even than the sadness of torture. Here, too, art participates in the drama of the Holy Whore.

2.

Given Fassbinder's certainty that the postwar order was "in for the duration," we should not be surprised to discover that the drama of the whore who would be holy is still all around us. It is quite familiar in fact, even if not much recognized for what it is. As Fassbinder said, "All you can do is keep your eyes open, and if you do, you certainly see the craziest things, if you look real hard" (135). The "crazy" thing in the present is that the drama is not the angst-filled problem of people who might actually like to be revolutionaries. So anxious is the ruling order about the very possibility of the holy (no matter how internally conflicted and difficult that quality has become) that it has appropriated the drama as something it can *sell*, can turn into *product*, and thus not only manage but render as a tidy *profit*. It's as if it said, "It's good that we can get revolutionaries to sell out, and better that we can make future revolutionaries self-conscious about the paradoxes of complicity. But in the best of all possible worlds we would be able to *create* our opposition, as something a priori sold out, as an enemy designed in our own image. If we must have enemies, let's create them ourselves and then turn them into business opportunities!"

Hence, "leftist" pop industries like *The Simpsons*. ("Doh! Why didn't I think of that?") What's most salient about *The Simpsons*— its occasional satire of American politics and culture or the endless line of products it makes profitable? To what degree do the products make the message irrelevant?

To take modestly loftier examples, during the last presidential campaign, at the end of a long and reckless first term made glorious by the son of George, discontent announced itself. Reclaim the left, we were urged by publishers and journals. New and crankier books by left-leaning authors Molly Ivins, Michael Moore, Al Franken, and others appeared. (Political movements now politely wait to announce themselves until the arrival of the new publishing season.) And of course we don't want to forget the ongoing selling of the presidency in the person of the latest liberal hope, Howard Dean, and his fearless denunciation of George Bush. How is that denunciation different from niche marketing? Because he's "sincere"? The reclaiming of the left is being marketed in the hope that the delusion of consumer activism or point-of-purchase revolution is still vital among us. So get out your Working Assets Master Card.

I will even confess (with a sort of craven, rueful glance heavenward) that my own book *The Middle Mind: Why Americans Don't*

Think for Themselves, was part of a promotional campaign in the fall of 2003 to "retake the left." Worse yet, from the first there was a whore at the heart of my work. *The book had to become what it criticized before it could exist at all.* The book's original "buzz" (without which it would never have gained the interest of its publisher) was the notoriety it received from being willing to "name names." In this case, I was willing to name another of America's hypermediated sweethearts, Terry Gross, as an example of my concept, the Middle Mind. She, I argued, is cultural middle management. She makes the claim of freshness where there is only more of the same. It is she who makes the implausible claim that we're thriving while around us everything is dead. This willingness to lampoon media figures like Gross created scandal. "No one ever says such things about Terry Gross!" I was told. A shiver of titillation became part of the book's promise to readers. I was persistently asked to comment on my criticism of Gross not because it was so hard to understand but because repeating the critique had something *lurid* about it. No matter what I wanted (a critique with real consequences), the public received what it wanted (another ephemeral scandal-commodity). In short, in order to critique a certain kind of fraud, I had to become part of that fraud.

This irony cuts so deep that I can feel it even in this moment of self-revelation. Isn't this aside itself a kind of product placement? Hey, buy my earlier book, *The Middle Mind*. This is like a can of Coke displayed prominently in a Hollywood movie. You know the cola wars. Meet the liberal left pundit war for market share. Brand name Curtis White in pursuit of brand name Michael Moore. People with product seek to achieve the equivalent of "liftoff": brand name recognition. Soon, I, too, might have a product line. Movie rights. Franchise rights. Middle Mind paraphernalia. *Bobblehead dolls!* Giggling endorsements from the right liberal celebrities. For example, Cameron Diaz might say, "When I take time away from my acting career to fight state power, I wear my Middle Mind decoding glasses. They cut through the media hype!"

So my book itself became the preeminent example of the thing it sought to critique! My desire to break a certain form only succeeded in affirming it and, worse yet, of *being* it. A large part of my point here is that there was absolutely nothing I could do about this. It was a mechanism beyond my control. The only thing I could do was keep my eyes open, as Fassbinder urged, and notice this "crazy thing," acknowledge it, and make it part of the next turn.

But, for the present, I should just go ahead and confess it. In spite of all appearances, I, too, am a holy whore.

The reclamation of the left in which I participated is indistinguishable from the contrary revolution on the right of people like Ann Coulter, Bill O'Reilly, Sean Hannity, Rush Limbaugh, and the inglorious rest (all of whom are perfectly happy to mesh their conservative revolutions with the needs of the marketing department). You have to wonder whether any of these bold political programs, whether right or left, are anything more than "gross national product." They are spectacles to which we are expected to pay admission. Some, like Christopher Hitchens, are shameless about their celebrity. "I was a leftist but now I hang with neo-cons. What difference does it make? I'm making a *lot* of money." Hitchens is a particularly frightening example because the political theater he inspires is sadomasochistic. People come to his lectures expecting to be insulted, and Hitchens never disappoints on that score. Whether on the left or right, figures like Hitchens are finally merely part of a large and very profitable market apparatus. It's called Culture War, but it could be more properly called Culture Theater. Nothing about his theater is at all serious about creating thought that would seek to work *outside* the market apparatus.

As an instance of this fraudulent theater and the easy opposition of liberal and conservative it makes available to us, consider Bill Maher (host of HBO's *Real Time with Bill Maher*). Maher is fond of apologizing for the frightening conservatism of Ann Coulter by saying, "I admire her. She says what she thinks." The problem, of course, is that anyone should think that what Ann Coulter does is thinking. Or what Bill Maher does, for that matter. What's "interesting" is that Maher and Coulter can pass for thinkers. (Now, that's a thought!) It's not because anyone actually expects to find live-on-camera thinking that they watch Maher's jejune productions. They watch because there is a giddy wonder, a lubricious glee, an info-pornographic fascination in the raw spectacle of people saying what they're not supposed to say. And yet the strange truth is that *by displaying people saying what they're not supposed to say, certain things are kept unsaid.*

Observe, if you will, the facial contortions of Larry King on his program of August 24, 2003, as Maher opined that priests molest boys because they became priests in the first place precisely because they like boys. There's nothing mysterious about it, for Maher. And certainly nothing complicated. Still, it pains the good Larry to hear these things that people aren't supposed to think, let alone say, and yet can't you just see a sort of shudder of pleasure mixed with that grimace of discomfort?

What, we ought to ask, is the consequence of such a moment? A jaded titillation out there in TV Land? At best one could perhaps report next day over the water cooler that "there was an interesting interview on *Larry King* last night." But for this we need a new definition of "interesting." Henceforth, *interesting* should mean "irrelevant," "impotent," and "feckless as the moon."

As Martin Heidegger put it in his little book *What Is Called Thinking?*

> Many people today take the view that they are doing great honor to something by finding it interesting. The truth is that such an opinion has already relegated the interesting thing to the ranks of what is indifferent and soon boring. (5)

And Heidegger could know this without the benefit of watching TV! From a philosopher's perspective, one of the sure signs that there's no thinking going on with Maher or Coulter or you-choose-the-pundit is that there is never a context for what they do. They are never thinking in the context of other thinkers. They are never reading, considering, interpreting what someone else has thought as a point of departure for what they think. It's all *ex nihilo*, as if ideas just burst in your head like an aneurysm.

Of course, these pundits do refer to each other, but that is no more than one end of the abyss calling to the other.

Still, as Maher has shown, it is true that there is in our culture a long list of things that can't be said. At least I imagine that it is a long list, but it's hard to be sure because obviously it's a list that is never said. In any event, so anxious are we about those things that can't be said that we have television programs like *Real Time* where people act out in a profane ritual what it might be like to say the things that can't be said, assuming that someone somewhere were ever to know those things and for some reason wanted to say them. On Maher's show, the drama is summoned with the provocative implication that it's "time to get real." Maher and Company provide their entirely passive audience with a *frisson*, the thrill of the illusion that the unspeakable is being spoken. That's why it's so wonderful to be an American! But if that freedom is a fraud? What then?

Magically, Maher accomplishes the tasks of getting real and saying things that can't be said without ever actually getting real or saying the things that can't be said . . . because Maher is finally in agreement that certain things shouldn't be said! In his book *When You Ride Alone, You Ride with Bin Laden*, Maher writes:

> Now, is there anything wrong with flags? Of course not. I like the flag plenty, but I never forget that it's only a symbol, a reminder of what we stand for, not a replacement for actually standing for it. Brave Americans in past wars didn't die for the actual flag—they died for the freedom it represents, including the freedom to burn it. (27)

Clearly, in the theater of popular politics Maher is taking an "extreme" and "liberal" stance on a "hot-button" issue: flag burning. The resoluteness of his position creates the far left side of the possible in public discourse. If you would say anything more than this, you are beyond the pale, one of the dogs that the polis release at night to roam the wilderness outside the city walls. Maher creates a limit beyond which one can only be a monster.

But look at how *near* this limit is. See how much he concedes to a position that I would take to be Coulter's as well.

1. I like the flag, and of course so should you.
2. It is a symbol of "what we stand for."
3. Brave Americans died for the freedom it represents.

Aside from Maher's permissive attitude toward flag burning, an utter red herring in his logic, he is otherwise asserting the most unspeakably hackneyed patriotic palaver. By defining a liberal extreme, Maher provides the limit of what will be tolerated. So, you'd better at least "like the flag plenty" (the mince-mouthed humbug!), you'd better believe that it "symbolizes" something, you'd better agree that we "stand for something," and you'd better believe that this something that we stand for and that is represented by the flag is "freedom."

Any undergraduate after a first course in analytic thinking could say that this is a textbook example of a question-begging tautology. It assumes what it should be proving, and it refers to nothing other than itself. Who is "we," Mr. Maher? Why can you blithely assume that "we" "stand for" some one thing? And what in the bleeding world do you mean by "freedom"? You probably mean what George Bush means, which means that you don't really mean anything at all by it. It is a concept utterly lacking in content. Yet Maher is the liberal extreme, banished by the networks to potty-mouthed HBO. But how *useful* he is. Abandon all hope of forgiveness, ye who would venture beyond him.

And what is it, you might ask, that these elaborate negations-in-the-form-of-affirmations finally forbid? What is the ultimate unsayable? That before which the entire political spectrum stands in horror? This thing that even putative liberals and conservatives condemn in unison, hand over beating heart? This thing that finds Republicans and Democrats arm in arm, one big flag over their collective shoulders?

It is this: You cannot say that the ruling order has no moral right to rule and hence no legitimacy. You cannot say that the order as a whole is *spiritually bankrupt*.

Let me put this another way, and this may seem to you truly unsayable. Federal governance in these theoretically United States is in a continuum with organized crime. In fact, it is probably a convenience that something like the Mafia exists, because if the Mafia is organized crime, maybe the federal government isn't. But the truth is conspicuous for anyone who wants to see. Business, politics, and legalized violence are a fluid whole. It's worth remembering that the symbol of the authority of the Roman consul was a bundle of rods (*fasces*) bound around an ax. The meaning of this authority was the right to kill in the name of the empire. It was to this tradition that the Italian fascists of the 1930s sought to return. (At least the fascists were open about their imperial purposes and their willingness to use violence to achieve them.) Similarly, in the United States, business interests and the violence of the state move effortlessly one into the other.

An example? Our ruthless vice president, former president of a large corporation (Halliburton), connived with the CIA to falsify evidence to legitimate a war in Iraq that made it possible for his corporation to profit from that war. We may not find WMDs (weapons of mass destruction), but finding AWPs (American war profiteers) is no problem. Go to Iraq (or Washington) and you'll trip over them. This is governance indistinguishable from organized violence for profit.

Or consider the work of Alliant Techsystems in Edina, Minnesota. They produce tank-buster shells made with depleted uranium. This radioactive material has sickened and killed thousands of Iraqis and American soldiers. Thanks to the work of Alliant, it should be no problem finding WMDs. Hold a Geiger counter anywhere that the American military has been, and you'll find our own WMDs. Or hold the Geiger counter to the urine of any American troop unfortunate enough to have been contaminated by our own weapons. Every depleted uranium bomb we drop is an attack on civilians *and* friendly fire.

On the other hand, Alliant's CEO took home $16.8 million in bonuses and stock options last year.[2] These examples are not aberrant, nor are they scandalous for Mr. Cheney or Alliant Techsystems.

They are merely *typical*. You should be able to conclude from them that the present ruling order has no right to rule, as Noam Chomsky has put it. But that's just the point, isn't it? Chomsky practically embodies those things-that-can't-be-said. So why isn't he on Bill Maher's program? Is it perhaps because he thinks that immoral governance is something more than material for late-night laughs? That maybe it's something we should act on?

One last comment on Bill Maher. If he likes Ann Coulter because she "says what she thinks" but what she does isn't thinking, then he needs to rephrase his comment. He should more properly say, "I admire Ann Coulter because she says things."

You know, I admire Bill Maher because he says things, too.

"Yeah, but what about Ann Coulter?" you might be worrying. "Isn't she dangerous? Doesn't someone need to confront her lies? Doesn't Maher do at least that for us?"

Probably not. She's a tar baby. She's tempting, but to attack her is to get stuck in a fight that is simply not the point. The real function of the opposition between Coulter and Maher is to create two sides to the cattle chute down which we're all funneled to one not very pleasant place of dumb self-love. If she still makes you nervous, let me provide you with a little visualization exercise.

When I was a student at the University of San Francisco in the late sixties, I would often walk down Haight Street just to see what sort of inspired nuttiness was going on. The place was a near ghetto at the time, the home not to the Gap but to what Frank Zappa called "psychedelic dungeons." Screwing up my courage, I'd occasionally duck into one of these dungeons out of curiosity. I once headed into a place claiming to be the headquarters for a religion through which one could attain physical immortality by committing (frequent) acts of anal intercourse of the homoerotic variety. (Sexist pig! What about immortality for women?) In the course of a not very long conversation with the male guru of this cult, I realized that I really had no way to prove to him that he was wrong. As he said, "You simply haven't tried it." I doubt that even the AIDS holocaust had much dissuasive power for him, assuming he lived that long.

Anyway, just imagine Ann and a little hand-painted sign reading "Slander! Treason! Liberal conspiracy!" out on Haight Street circa 1969. Now, don't go down those tempting steps into the dungeon. Just move on.

3.

In this section, I "bitch-slap" Al Franken. Actually, I borrow the language of "bitch slapping" from Franken himself, who gleefully relates in *Lies and the Lying Liars Who Tell Them* how he bitch-slapped Bernie Goldberg in public debate. It is so good that the pundits of liberalism have learned the idiom of the people. It disproves Ann Coulter's claim that liberals are elitists because they don't talk to truck drivers. It's also funny and shows that Franken and liberals are down with homies and shit. Honestly, this is how people who do their research at Harvard's Shorenstein Center on the Press, Politics, and Public Policy talk these days. Of course, seriously considered, neither the conservative populism of drinking beer with truck drivers nor the liberal politics of street cred are honest. Republicans do not care about working people (as their forever war against labor unions proves beyond all question), and Democrats do not finally care about the welfare of blacks (never mind legends about Clinton's genealogy). Whether Republican or Democrat, the two major political parties *always* leave the children of the poor behind.

Consider Detroit. Federal administrations of both parties come and go, but illiteracy in Detroit hovers around 50 percent. In a conversation with an administrator of the Detroit library system in 2003, I learned that the most eager private contributor to literacy in the city was McDonald's. And they were only concerned because the teenagers they were hiring couldn't even read the menu board. (Meanwhile, adult and child literacy in that most despised nation, Cuba, is nearly 100 percent.) Given the general indifference among politicians to realities of this kind, it is clear that the rhetorics of both parties are fraudulent. It is just as Chomsky says: they are both ultimately two sides to the one great Party of Business, and business has no interest in educating people it doesn't need. Which is the real message to the poor people of Detroit, a message they are not slow in understanding: "You are not needed. For anything. Ever. So why should we go to the trouble and expense of educating you?" When Wesley Clark says that the Democratic Party gives to the less fortunate out of spiritual conviction, that is true only in comparison with the practices of the Republicans. Otherwise, it is a lie.

In the end, to prefer a Democrat to a Republican is at best to prefer death by a thousand cuts to a good clean bullet to the base of the skull.

Let me just say it: Franken and Maher, two of the best-known, best-loved liberal heroes in the good fight against conservative extremism, are . . . conservatives. This is so if what is meaningful in their work is not its sporadic, spectacular, and scandalous opinions on hot-button issues like flag burning but simply a willingness to agree that there are limits to what can be said and thought and that those very limits precisely "conserve" the status quo, the two-party system, the reign of corporations, and the legitimacy of something called the "war against terror."

Do you feel the noose tightening?

Both Maher and Franken pledge their allegiance to the war against terror, but neither ever tries to unpack the historical amnesia and the cynicism contained within that thoughtless phrase. This is because to unpack that narrative opens the very credible possibility that our state is one of the "rogues." Could Franken or Maher imagine what Fassbinder suggested thirty years ago? "In the last analysis, terrorism is an idea generated by capitalism to justify better defense measures to safeguard capitalism" (Fassbinder, 37). They cannot say that, and they will not think such a thought, even if it means that to avoid thinking it they'll avoid thinking anything at all.

What Franken is willing to say is "I love America." With a little tear in his eye, no doubt. Franken argues that the biggest lie of conservatives is that "liberals hate America." But by replying that, no, liberals love America, too, Franken has created a political universe in which from end to end we all say, "I love America." It reminds me of the Huey Lewis song of some years back, "It's Hip to Be Square." It's liberal to be conservative! Franken can be one of these notorious liberals, *and* say "I love America." We used to call this sort of thing operating in "bad faith." In Franken's case, we might better say that it's "bad shtick."

What if you neither love America nor hate it? What if you simply don't have any idea what "America" is? Seriously, what *content* does the word contain for Franken? And what can it mean to say you "love" something that has no content? Is this America we love the land itself? Is it the prairies we've destroyed, the water and air we've polluted, and the species we've driven into extinction? Is it the forests we've clear-cut to make farmland, and the farmland that we've so depleted of nutrients that only by applying massive amounts of nitrogen (distilled from natural gas) can we get anything at all to grow in it? Or is our America the vinyl-clad subdivisions we erect on the depleted soil? If so, we "lovers" are dangerous. We're loving America to death. America should turn and run for cover when it sees us coming with our hungry arms outstretched.

Or perhaps it is our elected representatives that we mean when we say we "love America"? No one would believe that one. We at least have the good sense to hold our politicians in contempt no matter their party affiliation. Well, then, is it "the people" that we love? Perhaps, but not in any simple sense. The truth is that as a matter of habit and misconceived principle we cordially hate each other's guts on most days. Our national character is more riven than Sybil's personality. Religion, region, race, class, gender, and education all fracture us. We as a people are not one. And maybe it's a bad idea to try to be "one" (as our "united we stand" international militarism would seem to demonstrate).

Or—the ultimate possibility—is it perhaps the values expressed in our founding documents that we mean by "America"? I think most people would be willing to try to love those ideas, so long as the understanding is that those ideas have been only imperfectly realized and mostly require of us not some sort of sycophantic blind faith but a willingness to learn how to change.

It's enough to make you understand the joke that was circulating among Native Americans a few years back. The setup to the joke could be anything. You could say, "How do you get to Dallas?" You could say, "What's a television?" You could say, "Do you love America or hate it?" But the punch line was always the same: "White people are stupid." Then they'd laugh and laugh.

You know, instead of saying "I love America," I would prefer to say, *"Our democracy defends itself by appealing to values that make no sense but that we are not allowed to criticize."*

The bottom line here is that we live not simply in a free market economy; we live in a free market democracy ("the best democracy money can buy," as Greg Palast puts it). Nothing about "winning the war on terror" or "loving America" will change that basic reality one bit. You tell me how Al Franken touring with the USO or Bill Maher calling for broad citizen sacrifice in the war on terror makes them anything more than apologists for the status quo. They are conservative; they are opposed to fundamental change in a political system that is demonstrably corrupt, cruel, and functioning only in the interests of a small portion of its citizenry. The fact we have to face is that there is no domestic opposition to this system that is *radical* in the sense that it is willing to get to the *root* of our problems. The Maher/Coulter Franken/O'Reilly oppositions are nothing more than public spectacle, political circus, the semblance of difference where there is none. They are the whores that the system itself nominates as holy, as the authentic "revolutionary" spirits of the left and right. In the final analysis, they are product and they are wildly profitable. They are the summons to fundamental change that means everything will stay exactly the same.

4.

What is refreshing and tonic in Fassbinder's strategy of the Holy Whore, as a politic and a poetic, is that its purpose was to make itself *useless*, useless to the left and useless to the right. Nevertheless, this uselessness provided dissonance in a world created for the convenience of exchange and profit. Fassbinder's hope was that simply acknowledging the whore at the heart of liberalism could make the system stumble. Fassbinder's refusal to confirm or conform always sought to leave the future *open*.

In our present political situation, the confidence game in the name of which the likes of Ann Coulter and Al Franken collude, the future is not open largely because their fraudulent drama does not acknowledge its collusion with the present order of things. Whether we consider ourselves liberal or conservative, a "fan" of Franken or of Coulter, the future must look an awful lot like the past. We need to "reclaim the left" not as a marketing ploy but as a fundamental demand. Capitalism has successfully given birth to its god: the Market. But it is, in Thomas Frank's phrase, a "God that sucks." Corporate capitalism accumulates power not in order to spend it in a vision of a human world but only in order to hoard it. It seeks only to maintain its structures and privileges. Its decadence is a reflection of the fact that it has no idea what to do with the authority it has claimed except to indulge itself. Tom DeLay corrupts his office and exposes himself to federal prosecutors in order to go golfing in Scotland? Randy Cunningham becomes a felon in order to buy a big boat that practically screams, "I am graft! Put me in jail!"? That's the best thing they can think to do with the power they have accumulated? In our turn, we need to *refuse* the *sterility* of the reign of money in the name of the freeing of our own creativity.

The self-criticism of the Holy Whore needs to be a new start and not a reason for despair, fatalism, and paralysis. After all, no political pessimism halted Fassbinder's artistic productivity (although drugs, alcohol, and a generally disdainful attitude toward health did). We need self-criticism, but we also need strategies for hope, for maintaining the reality if not the imminence of *the possible*. So, I come to it again, what if we stopped thinking of our primary moral law as the Golden Rule of "love thy neighbor"? As I have tried to show, that law has been made subject to an institutional framework of "justice" that means only evil. What if we tried to think our lives and to act according to an ethic concerned, rather, with what we would willingly give to the future? How would we think that thought? How is it possible to think that thought in our present weird "institutionalized isolation" in which we are splendidly "alone together," our smiley-faced version of solitary confinement? (I ask this from the pleasant isolation of my study, before my Macintosh computer, in the middle of a midsize Illinois town, in the middle of the North American continent. Zoom back. Planet Earth. Vast and chaotic interstellar reaches.) In short, how do "we" become a "we" with a common creative future and not a future that we can look up in a programming guide?

As I have said, this requires a *socialized* strategy of refusal of the "life"-in-progress. I emphasize the word *socialized* because the real problem is not reclaiming life for you or me. I think that's perfectly possible for an individual even in the present context. The real issue is how to make a living community. The refusal takes place in the moment that a counterspirit to the spirit of capitalism articulates a demand. For instance, rather than attacking the "elite" privilege of research creativity for college professors like myself, why not, as I suggested earlier, demand an approach to daily life that includes the opportunity for creativity for everyone? This is a simple suggestion revealing a pathological dysfunction in our culture, but for most of us it is almost unthinkable.

A demand for the opportunity of creativity for all citizens is opposed to the reigning assumption that work is supposed to be drudgery but you do it anyway, in order to care for your family, and so the sacrifice of your own adult life becomes a sort of virtue. We're told by politicians, pundits, and parents, "You should be grateful that you have a job at all." No one thinks in these late days of Global Capital Triumphant as Paul Goodman thought in his book *Growing Up Absurd*:

> *Nobody* asks if a job is useful or honorable (within the limits of business ethics). A man gets a job that pays well, or well enough, that has prestige, and good conditions, or at least tolerable conditions. . . . But *the question is what it means to grow up*

onto such a fact as: "During my productive years I will spend eight hours a day doing what is no good." (29)

A demand for work that is "good" is the expression of hope. It is the expression of a claim on the future: this is a world I could willingly live in as a fully human world. It does not deny the Golden Rule, but it is "beyond" it insofar as its interests are so much more social, so much more *constructive*—that is, so much more about *making*. This is a Nietzschean impulse. As even Nietzsche understood, Jesus's commandment to love was an expression of strength. "Jesus said to his Jews: 'The law was for servants—love God as I love him, as his Son! What have we Sons of God to do with morals!'" (469). Jesus's commandment to love is thus not merely an admonition to the strong to do no harm to the weak, and it is certainly not about justice as Old Testament retribution (this notion of justice has done nothing more than allow us to criminalize people who have been systematically impoverished, and to warehouse the unruly poor in prisons). It is the affirmative compulsion to act in the world, with strength, in the name of the Good. Call it beauty. Call it health. What is "beyond good and evil" is the demand that the human world be allowed to thrive. It is the demand for creativity, play, and beauty in the most serious sense. It is, in Slavoj Žižek's phrase, the "work of love." Given a Nietzschean spin, Jesus's commandment is the appeal to seize the world in the *strength* of love.

What is so perverse about the world as it stands is that the only humans who claim this human right to world making are corporate capitalists who in fact do make the world over in their own image, but it is the image of a sort of death. The strip mall is capitalist world making. The strip mine is capitalist world making. The terrible fascist beauty of our military machine is capitalist world making. To admire the beauty of a weapon—whether a gun or a fighter jet—is to think like a fascist, and, unhappily, nearly every movie and every television drama encourages us, and especially the children among us, to experience weapons as beautiful. Every time Hollywood or television shows us a gun, it says, "This is a beautiful thing." Glock; .38 caliber; Smith and Wesson; Uzi; Kalashnikov.

Beautiful. Our so-called air shows are really just an indulgence in war porn. They exalt the beauty of the fighter jet, quite distanced from the way in which that jet is experienced in the hinterlands of the empire, where its roaring approach sounds only like the most iniquitous death. In such a world the "great yea to life" that was both Nietzsche's and Jesus's is utterly lacking.

The demand for the right to work that is not immediately a confirmation of the capitalist imagination is not dreamily utopic because making it a living reality is so easy to articulate. In the 1970s, Congressman Donald M. Fraser from Minnesota actually proposed that a sabbatical system be created for all working Americans through which up to three times in their lifetime, they could take up to a year of sabbatical time to pursue their own educational or professional or spiritual or merely idiosyncratic interests by drawing on their own Social Security accounts. This was only "unrealistic" because business interests bitterly opposed it. In reality, its financial plausibility was easy to show. Just as it works in universities, workers with seniority can be temporarily replaced with cheaper labor. Sabbaticals can actually save money for universities, and they could be made to save money for businesses as well. In fact, it would even be worth it to employers to pay into the sabbatical program for reasons that are not just fiscal but that include health, job-related innovation, family well-being, and worker loyalty. Nonetheless, the idea of replacing a work ethic of drudgery with work that provides the general opportunity for creativity is viewed with horror by nearly *everyone*, boss and worker alike. (How sad is that?)

And yet the future is claimed in creative ways by many of us all the time. It is all around us but it is a minority affair, to be sure. An obvious example: if you refuse to shop at Wal-Mart and participate instead in a local organic food co-op or simply shop at a local natural foods store, you are participating in the spirit and the ethic I am trying to describe as a practical and (I would go so far as to say) *revolutionary* response to the present. You are creating a human demand on the future. You are saying, "Die, Sam's Club. Wither away." On a larger scale, the Organic Valley farmer co-op, begun in

1988 in La Farge, Wisconsin, now includes more than six hundred farmers in sixteen states. Its sales of $156 million in 2003 were up 25 percent over 2002. Beyond its profitability, this business is, in very simple terms, an expression of a refusal of the dominant reality of American agribusiness and an appeal to a very different future. It is *pious*, it is *hopeful*, and it is *compassionate*. It is also ornery and determined, as any such quixotic enterprise must be. That is, its real motivating ethic is a desire that farmers, consumers, and the natural world should cease suffering at the hands of an agricultural economy that is nothing short of toxic and cruel in its disdain for the health and economic well-being of farmers, consumers, and the environment. Agribusiness is rapacious and pitiless. Organizations like Organic Valley sustain a culture of refusal of the corporate present and they propose an alternative future.

Real though this example is, it sure is not something that the media tries to foreground for us. It is ideologically invisible. Organic farming struggles on as an expensive niche tucked away in a corner of the local supermarket or available only to affluent and educated consumers through franchised (and decidedly upscale) stores like Wild Oats Markets. The difficulty with an operation like Wild Oats is that as it grows as a corporation (now over one hundred stores in twenty-five states and Canada), its original mission is challenged by the logic of "market share." The more successful it is, the more attractive it becomes to larger corporate entities, and the more it has to behave like those entities in order to survive their interest. That semidivine thing referred to as the Market has in fact recognized the profitability of organic farming and has assumed responsibility for broadening the revolution that Organic Valley and Wild Oats began. But competition from large agricultural businesses like Dole (which has moved into the organic salads area) will mean increasing competition for businesses like Organic Valley in the near future. If in the end Dole's economics of size allow it to squeeze producers like Organic Valley out of the market, we may have organic food to eat, and our health may be incrementally improved, but the Organic Valley *spiritual* revolution will have been lost. This is because the only virtue that provokes Dole's participation in the field is profit. When it has booted businesses like Organic Valley from the competition, profit will be the only virtue determining the future of farming, just as it has for the last half-century of ruin for the family farm, the environment, and us, the people who eat the food. Piety, hope, and compassion are not on the agenda at Dole's stockholder meetings.

Worse yet, this likely battle over market share between idealists and corporations is really only a niche market. Because of the added expense of producing "green" products, businesses have no choice but to try to sell them to people who can *afford* to have a social conscience. As Heather Rogers, author of *Gone Tomorrow: The Hidden Life of Garbage*, puts it:

> If you've got a company and you've decided to go green, it's going to cost more. You're going to be competing with companies that aren't doing that, and aren't incurring the greater cost. Either that's going to drive you out of business, or into the realm of manufacturing luxury items to sell to people who have now embraced this whole new level of consumption that's connected to organic living, organic lifestyles. But those goods aren't available to working class families or to people who live in public housing. Those are high-end consumer items. So, that kind of change is not going to affect a greater change across the board.[3]

The argument that the Market Knows Best is perhaps the most familiar and most mystified piece of common economic wisdom of the moment. It is the mantra of Free Market neo-cons, those who, like Francis Fukuyama, have declared that history is ended and that the world is presently as good as we have any right to expect, and we have Free Markets to thank for that fact. For them, the refusal of a culture of death in the name of a living future is a perverse thing. An unnecessary thing. The world is good, just, creative, and beautiful as it stands. It's a kind of paradise, as David Brooks's *Bobos in Paradise* suggests. It has even made the most common household items, like our toilets, into objects of aesthetic gratification, as Virginia Postrel argues in *The Substance of Style*. In her most recent

93

book, *The Future and Its Enemies*, Postrel goes so far as to claim that Free Market "dynamists" are the true "party of life."

> Today we have greater wealth, health, opportunity, and choice than at any time in history—the fruits of human ingenuity, curiosity, and perseverance. Yet a chorus of intellectuals and politicians loudly laments our condition. Technology, they say, enslaves us. Economic change makes us insecure. Popular culture coarsens and brutalizes us. Consumerism despoils the environment. The future, they say, is dangerously out of control, and unless we rein in these forces of change and guide them closely, we risk disaster.[4]

Neo-cons are, in short, adopting the spiritual rhetoric of "life," the emancipatory rhetoric of "creativity," and the romantic rhetoric of "beauty" for their description of the Free Market status quo, never mind the evidence to the contrary, and never mind that Postrel's description could at best apply to those in the top 10 percent of income (those that Brooks describes as Bobos—bourgeois bohemians). In the end, Postrel and Brooks are right only if we first accept the scapegoating of the majority of the population who are given only a future defined by low-paying service sector jobs, the demise of quality public education, and a debased popular culture of "reality" TV, violent cinema, and violent and sexist computer games. In short, they are given a future best described in programs like *COPS*.

In the next two chapters, I will, first, look at how the Thoreauvian tradition of the "spirit of disobedience" is in thorough disagreement with neo-cons like Postrel. Next, I will look at some of those among us who are not merely asserting that the future is open but actively *living* that future in the present, and as much outside the market apparatus as they can manage. They act, and encourage us to act, as if the present world were already ended, not because, as Fukuyama has it, history has ended but because the future beckons. They argue, "This is what I'd give the future if I could." Theirs is an ethic of creativity and *becoming*.

Chapter 4

The Spirit of Disobedience

The great epochs in our life are at the points when
we gain courage to rebaptize our badness as the
best in us.

—Nietzsche, *Beyond Good and Evil*

1.

According to most media commentators, the great contemporary moral and political question is, Are we fun-
damentally a Christian or an Enlightenment culture? Boards of
education in states like Kansas and Missouri rock from election to
election between advocacy of a Christian doctrine of "intelligent
design" and a secular and scientific commitment to evolution. In
editorial pages across the country, ordinary people earnestly debate
whether it was the intention of the Founding Fathers (whose authority is second only to God's in these matters) to found a Christian nation. These grassroots debates often seem merely silly and ill
informed (the comical idolatry for these "Fathers"; the failure to
understand that most of them were Deists). Nonetheless, this division in our character often has deep and troubling consequences, as
reports in the news occasionally make clear. For instance, consider the
article filed by Kirk Johnson of the *New York Times* on March 28, 2005.
He reports that Colorado's Supreme Court threw out the sentence
of a man who had been given the death penalty because jurors had
consulted the Bible in reaching a verdict. The court argued that the

jury should have avoided "outside influences" like newspaper arti-
cles, television programs, or, in this case, the Bible. Rather, the court
expected jurors to possess, in Johnson's wording, "internal codes of
right and wrong." On the one hand, what is astonishing here is the
idea that "legal experts" imagine that human beings possess something called "internal codes." Are these legal experts in fact neo-
Kantians assuming the existence of categories of moral duty
located in that part of the brain once called the Reason? On the
other hand, one has to acknowledge that it is equally surprising, if
even more naive, to imagine that jurors could consult the Bible for
unambiguous moral guidance. If you read Leviticus, you get one
answer; if you read Matthew, you get another. String him up or
turn the other cheek? Flip a coin? But most naive of all is the idea
that these so-called internal codes that jurors are encouraged to
consult could be imagined to be innocent of biblical influence. Not
in this culture, they couldn't. It isn't enough to say that the court's
decision is incoherent, which it certainly is. What's important is
that the incoherence so perfectly captures a national confusion
about the relation of Christian to Enlightenment thought.

What's doubly strange is that we should follow with such fascination and intensity this old dispute over our national character
while entirely ignoring the dominant ethos of our culture for the
last two hundred years. It should go without saying that it is capitalism that most defines our national character, not Christianity or
the Enlightenment. (Adam Smith's *Wealth of Nations*—with its ar-
guments for the good of the division of labor, the good of money,
and the preeminent good of free trade—was published, after all, in
1776.) As H. O. Havemeyer, president of the sugar trust, acknowledged in 1899 (a time, apparently, when businessmen were more
frank about such things), "Business is not a philanthropy. . . . I do
not care two cents for your ethics. I don't know enough of them to
apply them. . . . As a business proposition it is right to get all out of
a business that you possibly can" (Kirkland, 320). Or, as John Kenneth Galbraith put it, "We have for long had a respected secular
priesthood whose function it has been to rise above questions of

ethics, kindness and compassion and show how these might have to be sacrificed on the altar of the larger good" (290).

And so as the judge and jury in Colorado struggle with the confusion over what system of ethical values to apply to a case, the very nature of the system in which they function goes unexamined. It is, I hardly need to rehearse, a system in which poor people are at a grotesque disadvantage. (The full grotesqueness of this disadvantage was dramatically demonstrated by Hurricane Katrina when that 40 percent of the New Orleans population living beneath the poverty line literally floated to the surface of national consciousness.) Justice, under capitalism, works not from a notion of obedience to moral law, or to conscience, or to compassion, or even to "internal codes," but from the assumption of a duty to preserve a social order and the legal "rights" that constitute that order, especially the right to property and the freedom to do with it what one wants. That's the real and important "internal code" sought by our courts. It comes to this: that decision will seem most just which preserves the system of justice even if the system is itself routinely unjust.

Capitalism has not believed and does not believe in the authority of Jesus's spiritual vision, nor does it feel constrained by Kant's Enlightenment ethic which argued that human beings should be treated as ends not means. It can't even be said to believe in utilitarianism's calculating approach to benefit: "the greatest good for the greatest number." Such a precept causes capitalism a sort of painful suspicion that it might distract it from the immediate goal of maximizing profit. "Just how many of these others do I have to benefit? I understand that I am not the keeper of my brothers, at least not all of them, but why should I keep *any* of them?"

Most of what we perceive to be the social losses, the reversals of New Deal social programs, under the Reagan/Bush revolutions is simply capitalism adjusting in its own favor the sliding scale of utilitarian benefit. And so in late 2005 Congress could enact $50 million in cuts to social programming for the poor in the name of "deficit reduction" while enacting $90 million in tax cuts that will help only the already affluent. "That's enough help for the poor," capitalism says in effect. "The rest are on their own." In the end, it only believes in the sanctity of profitable returns to stockholders to whom there is no greater pledge of moral fealty, if one is to believe our nation's chief executive officers. That is the only certain morality of the Free Market. "Our stockholders deserve a return on the investment they have entrusted with us and we are honor-bound to maximize that return," say our captains of industry on CNBC or Fox or *Wall Street Week* or even *The Nightly Business Report* on PBS, a little tear of commitment welling in the corner of their eyes. They do not trouble themselves to try to operate under what John Ruskin called "conditions of moral culture," whether Christian or Enlightenment. Compassion is at most something for private consideration as charity, although even that must be made economically rational as a tax deduction.[1]

And yet in spite of all of this that should be evident to any half-attentive American, capitalism has managed somehow to convince the people subject to it that in fact the truest religious people (the *real* Christians, as they think) are its strongest advocates. Of course, it is no secret to say that in the United States the assumption is that Christians are Republicans and the Republican Party is the party of capitalism writ large. As the Reverend Chan Chandler of East Waynesville Baptist Church, North Carolina, has made clear, if you don't vote Republican, you're in the way of "God's work," and you'll be asked to leave the church.[2]

As a consequence, our political options have been turned into a deadly game of either/or. You're either a Christian Republican or a secular Democrat. Revelation or Reason. The extremity and the irresolvability of this division is, if not clear to ourselves, obvious to those outside our fold. In an article in the British magazine *The Economist*, the following revealing statistics are emphasized.[3] According to a survey conducted by the University of Pennsylvania's National Annenberg Election survey, 36 percent of registered voters in Republican Missouri identify themselves as born-again Christians, while just 6 percent so identify in Democratic Massachusetts. *The Economist* concludes, "The Republicans are becoming the party of committed Christians, the Democrats that of committed secularists.

The 2004 election could well turn into a choice between Michael Moore's *Fahrenheit 9/11* and Mel Gibson's *The Passion of the Christ*."

This assumption about the nature of partisan division is increasingly common on our own shores as well. For example, Susan Jacoby's recent book *Freethinkers: A History of American Secularism* is an only just barely concealed partisan attack on evangelical Republicans by "reasonable," freethinking Democrats. And the title of former secretary of labor Robert Reich's book says it all: *Reason: Why Liberals Will Win the Battle for America.*

But it is strange that this opposition should seem so new and newsworthy to us. We have lost sight of just how *old* these differences are. In early postcolonial America, there was already a division between the "coast and the hinterlands," in Van Wyck Brooks's phrase. In the hinterlands, Puritan discipline and extremity still reigned, and the fire and brimstone preaching of the new evangelical orders (inspired by Methodism's John Wesley) was on the rise. But on the coast, the "Boston religion," Unitarianism, had triumphed and exerted a great liberalizing and moderating influence on American life and thought. It was the coastal elitism of enlightened self-reliance led by Harvard College versus the abject rural conviction of sinfulness before an angry God. Sound familiar? And yet this is a description of 1820.

Neither is it a strictly American problem. When, during the French Revolution, the new republic nationalized the property of the Catholic Church in the name of the natural rights of man (and, not incidentally, to raise resources to pay off the national debt of Louis XVI), they created what was called the "two Frances." In essence, one of the earliest and most controversial decisions of the new republic divided what was then called the "third estate" (what we would call the "general public") between those who had been persuaded by Voltaire and the *philosophes* and those who remained loyal to the Catholic Church.

We can even go back to the origins of the Reformation, 1517. As Jacques Barzun writes of the antagonism between the Lutherans and the advocates of Erasmus's "Christian humanism," "The Evangelicals despised the Humanists." Strange though it may sound, our own red state/blue state dilemma is really this old and generalized throughout Western culture.[4]

Still, the ironies of the present are many and profound and not to be explained away by a sense of historical inevitability. Do Democrats really imagine that they can articulate a compelling moral vision for the United States or for the democratic West without a spiritual foundation? Does Robert Reich imagine that he can succeed where Kant and the Enlightenment failed, in establishing an ethics and a politics of Reason? Or, worse, do Democrats really imagine they can compete with Republican evangelicals by becoming more like them? Shall we all talk about our born-again justification in the body of Jesus? Shall we all head down to the river to collect our votes?[5]

Or, ironies for the other side, do Christian Republicans really not understand the fundamental ways in which an unfettered corporate capitalism betrays Jesus's ethical vision *and* their own economic well-being? (It is an astonishing irony that these religious anti-Darwinians are in their politics and economics the most uncompromising social Darwinians with a naive and self-defeating assumption of the virtue of competition. Of course, the people of "lowest development" to be "weeded out," as Herbert Spencer put it, are demonstrably themselves!) Most fantastically, do Christian Republicans really not recognize their own perverse marriage with secular rationalism? There is an unacknowledged alliance between the pragmatic and ultra-rational needs of corporate capitalism with the blarney of Christian cleansing through the "social values" movement. What other possible explanation is there for the Bush-Cheney popular victory in 2004? Wholly secular technorationalists in business and the military were just as happy with the Bush-Cheney victory as were value-driven fundamentalist Christians. On November 4, 2004, while churches rejoiced and sang hosannas in praise of God's good work in the reelection strategy, Wall Street was "set to soar" (Reuters) and the Dow bounced up over one hundred points.

In the end, Christianity conspires with technical and economic rationalism. In the end, they both require a commitment to "duty" that masks unspeakable violence and injustice. In the end, the Muslim whose legs are being reduced to pulp by his American tormentor doesn't care if he's being murdered because he is despised by Christians or because he is an impediment to economic rationality. He understands far better than we do how the two become one at the end of the torturer's rod. The Predator missile, product of American scientific ingenuity, that homes in on his head is both self-righteously and arrogantly evangelical and meanly pragmatic. It is the empire that the rest of the world reads in George Bush's smirk. The only meaningful question, as John Ruskin understood 150 years ago, is determined by "fraud in peace and force in war": who is to die and how? (*Munera*, 7).

The great emblem of this marriage between rationality and religion is, of course, Wal-Mart. In the Age of Wal-Mart (as a November 2004, CNBC television documentary put it), meetings of store managers are held in arenas. These conventions look like revival meetings, they feel like revival meetings, and I suspect that most of the participants would be quite comfortable in thinking that they are revival meetings. But they're not kidding anybody. Wal-Mart is about two things: price and profit. It is rational in the meanest sense. Wal-Mart is the future not only of economic rationalism but of American religiosity as well.

Ruskin wrote of capitalist wealth that, "the cruelest man living could not sit at this feast, unless he sat blindfolded" (*Unto This Last*, 38). And yet at the feast that is Wal-Mart, ordinary people greet rationalized cruelty with shouts of thanksgiving.

Worst and most strangely of all, this powerful and apparently inevitable national opposition between the secular and the sacred, the reality on which all national and local political strategies will be balanced, is an opposition in name only. It is national theater. It is sameness masquerading as difference. Finally, and most critically, this opposition *excludes at all levels* any meaningful questioning of the desirability of global corporate capitalism. Democrat or Republican, liberal or conservative, secular or sacred, we're all in the Great Party of Business, and we're all doing its work. The rest is sound and fury signifying if not nothing then something very different from what we imagined.

Our firm assumption that our culture war is only about evangelicals and secular humanists means not only that the ethos of capitalism will escape scrutiny, will pass as if it were as innocent and inevitable as the air we breathe, but also that it will be nearly impossible to suggest an alternative to this opposition. By making concrete the hostility between the secular and the sacred, the scientific and the religious, in American consciousness, and making the idea of an alliance between them seem laughable, we have created a binarism as fundamental as the opposition between good and evil. This binarism tolerates no other players. Never mind, as I have said, that these two mortal enemies are really capable of the most earnest conspiracy. Never mind that our Christian evangelicals are free market Christians for whom economic rationality always trumps compassion. While they dominate the stage, no other player may make any claim for our attention.

If we live in a "culture of death," as Pope John Paul II put it, it is a culture that is made possible by the advocates of both Reason and Revelation. In the opposition of Reason to Revelation, Death cannot lose. Ours is a culture in which death has taken refuge in a legality that is supported by both reasonable liberals and Christian conservatives. Our exploitation of humans as "workers" is legal and somehow, weird and perverse though it may seem, generally acknowledged as part of our heritage of freedom, and virtually the entire political spectrum falls over itself to praise it. When Wal-Mart pays its employees impoverishing wages without adequate health or retirement benefits, we justify it out of respect for Wal-Mart's "freedom," its "reasonable" need to make itself "competitive," and because what it does is legal. As George Whalin, president of Retail Management Consultants put it, "They don't have a responsibility to society to pay a higher wage than the law says you have to pay."[6]

Similarly, our use of the most fantastically destructive military power is also legal and also somehow a part of our heritage of "protecting freedom" no matter how obscene and destructive its excesses (and it is almost *all* excess). The grotesque violence of video games and Hollywood movies, doing God knows what to the "internal codes of right and wrong" of teenagers, is legal and somehow now a protected part of our freedom of expression. (Military recruiters increasingly depend on this ethical God-knows-what as they hand out free graphically violent video games like the U.S. Army's own "America's Army" or Kuma's "Fallujah: Operation al-Fajr" to potential recruits. It is here that teenagers first learn of the thrill and satisfaction of "getting my kills," as our soldiers-in-arms put it these days.)

Even, as the more thoughtful antiabortionists complain with some justice, the legality of abortion at times covers an attitude toward human life that subjects life to the low logic of efficiency and what is convenient. The idea of abortion as a minor "out-patient medical procedure" becomes Orwellian in its intense determination not to "know what we do."

Or, perhaps most destructively, the legality of property rights condemns nature itself to annihilation even as we call it the freedom to pursue personal happiness and prosperity through the ownership of private property. This legality formalizes and empowers our famous "unalienable right" to property (especially that most peculiar form of private property known as the corporation), the exercise of which will profoundly "alienate" those on whom this right is inflicted: workers, children, foreign enemies, and animals.

In its most extreme and universal form, our constitutional rights are reducible to the right not to have to love our neighbor. The irony is that the more energetically we pursue our individual, socially isolated right to "life, liberty, and the pursuit of happiness," the deader the social and natural worlds become. The freedom we practice is, in Marx's phrase, an "unconscionable freedom."

2.

For all the inevitability that surrounds the Christian/Enlightenment divide, it should not be so difficult for us to find a third option in our intellectual traditions, even if this tradition seems mostly defeated and lost in the present. It is a tradition that is spiritual yet hostile to the orthodoxies of institutional Christianity. It is the creation of the Enlightenment, and yet it is suspicious of the claims of Reason, especially that form of reason, economic rationalism, that defines capitalism. This tradition began, in Europe, with Rousseau and romanticism and, in America, with the Concord transcendentalists. Together they created a sort of "counter-Enlightenment" in the West. (It was Rousseau who initiated this reaction by challenging Voltaire's Reason in the name of Feeling.) Near its origin is the poetic system devised by William Blake in the late eighteenth century. In this system there was, to be sure, condemnation of the backward-looking institution of the Christian church, but there was also condemnation of the figure of Enlightenment rationalism, what Blake called Ratio. Christianity, for Blake, bled from Jesus his real substance as prophet-poet. Reason, or Ratio, on the other side, born with the scientific revolution, divided the world from the self, the human from the natural, the inside from the outside, and the outside itself into ever finer degrees of manipulable parts. From Blake's point of view, both religion and Reason were deeply antihuman, deeply destructive errors.

Blake's third term, the place he called home, was the Imagination. Blake's use of the Imagination is not exotic. Ralph Waldo Emerson's richly American thought was deeply dependent on the Romantic tradition that Blake began. Sounding every bit the descendant of Blake, Emerson wrote in his essay "Self-reliance," "the inquiry leads us to that source, at once the essence of genius, of virtue, and of life, which we call Spontaneity or Instinct. We denote this primary wisdom as Intuition, whilst all later teachings are tuitions" (*Essential*, 141). For Emerson as well as Blake, Jesus was the supreme prophet and poet who had realized the full creative capacities of every human. In the church, on the other hand, "the soul is not preached" (*Essential*, 71). In the church, our instincts are trampled. The church is a dead thing.

As shocking as these ideas still sound to us, they represent a fundamental American tradition that ought to be as much a part of our usable heritage as the moral severity that was left to us by Cotton Mather and Jonathan Edwards and that is preached to this day by the Jerry Falwells of the world and implemented with extremity (and cynicism) by politicians like former Texas representative Tom DeLay. In contrast to institutional Christianity, whether dull Unitarians or fiery evangelicals, Emerson imagined that the world is held together by a spirit that is not of the church, and certainly not of Reason, but of a direct experience of the world. Emerson made this Romantic idea American, and he gave it first to Henry David Thoreau, then to Walt Whitman, and through Whitman to Ezra Pound, Charles Olson, Allen Ginsberg, and so many fractured movements of the recent past and present: the sixties counterculture, the environmental movement with its deep respect for nature, and New Age spiritualism, in particular. They are the heirs to the Imagination's counter-Enlightenment, with its contempt for the hierarchical authority of the church and its deep suspicion of what was unleashed by Enlightenment Reason.

As Hegel famously suggested, speaking of phrenologists in particular and empiricism in general, some people are capable of regarding a bone as reality. In the absence of the Imagination, our sense of the real has ossified. It's like a great thigh bone on the ends of which are our inevitable bulbous realities-in-opposition, the Christian and Scientific worldviews. What the Imagination seeks is an opportunity. It seeks a moment when the dry bone of the real is just for a moment "out of joint," as Shakespeare's Hamlet puts it, so that it can assert its difference. In the fraudulent Manichaeism of Reason and Revelation, each the light to the other's dark, each more like the other than it knows, the Imagination seeks to be a decisive rupture.

Henry David Thoreau found his time so much out of joint that he concluded that it was better to cease to exist than to continue in corruption and injustice. As he writes in "On the Duty of Civil Disobedience": "The people must cease to hold slaves, and to make war on Mexico, though it cost them their existence as a people" (225). For Thoreau, the moral bearing of the state reached a point where he was forced to conclude "we are no longer our self" (just as Hamlet concluded that Denmark was not Denmark but "something rotten").

As a consequence, Thoreau was not a citizen of the state of Massachusetts any more than Hamlet was, in the end, a Dane. As Thoreau put it in a statement to his town clerk, "Know all men by these presents, that I, Henry Thoreau, do not wish to be regarded as a member of any incorporated society which I have not joined" (233). For Thoreau, when the time was out of joint, when the state had failed its own idea of itself, he felt a necessity to remove himself from it, to refuse its social order, in spite of the personal price he would have to pay for the gesture. What's striking in the example that Thoreau offers us is how familiar his enormous and tragic sense of *betrayal* is. For us, too, things seem out of joint. America is not America. When the Bush-Cheney administration orchestrated a war in Iraq, many of us said, and continue to say, "not in my name." This is the equivalent of saying "Your society is not one that I have willingly joined. You may not proceed as if I were one with you."

This gesture of self-alienation is the first moment of disobedience. But we should see that it is not a "revolutionary" disobedience. Thoreau's disobedience is disobedience as refusal. I won't live in your world. I will live as if your world has ended, as indeed it deserves to end. *I will live as if my gesture of refusing your world has destroyed it.* Or we might say, hopefully, as Paul says in Corinthians I, that "the present form of the world is passing away." Thoreau's famous retreat to Walden Pond is thus in a continuum with his sense of the duty of disobedience. He argued that in "a government which imprisons any unjustly, the true place for a just man is also a prison" (230). Less self-destructively, we might say that Thoreau concluded that you might find a just man *outside*, at Walden Pond, in a self-created exile that is also the expression of a desire for the *next* world. He understood this exile as the need to create a society— even if a society of one on the banks of a tiny Massachusetts pond—which he could willingly join.

Henry David Thoreau's idea of disobedience is not only about an antisocial unruliness; it is also the expression of a desire for the spiritual. In this he is unlike the tradition of secular liberalism that has failed us so miserably (and so recently) in the policies and campaigns of the Democratic Party. It is not about a purely secular or political ethic that "reasonable" legislators can take care of if we can just elect the right people, especially since the legality they would confer would surely also have about it the stink of death. Thoreau's disobedience is most about *spirit*.

Walden is a work of Jesus-like thinking. That is, Thoreau was intent on confronting a culture that he perceived as being death-in-life with an appeal to life both temporal and transcendental. In the end, Thoreau was not interested only in making economies with his little handmade household on Walden Pond; he was just as interested in making eternity. Thoreau has something critical to teach us, if we'd let him, about the relation of the personal to the public and of the spiritual to the political. But he's mostly not available to us. He is shut away with a lot of other books in the virtuous and therapeutic confines of literary and historic institutions. He peers out to us from the pages of his book as another defeated man—another dead white man, as the professors say these days. Our question is whether we any longer know how to retrieve our own traditions from their institutional entombment. This can't be done by teaching *Walden* in high school. "Saved" by the American literary canon, Thoreau is mere dead letter. Thoreau can only be retrieved if we find a way to integrate his thought into the way we live as a sort of counterlife opposed to the busy work of the legality of the culture of death. But what is his thought? How would he argue to us if he could?

Thoreau was no Marxist, but he was, like Marx, appalled by what work did to human beings. And by and large Thoreau was aware of this human damage without the benefit of experiencing the grim reality of the nineteenth-century English factory. Most of his examples are agrarian, and so his conclusions surprise us, his twenty-first-century readers, because we tend to look back at our agrarian past as a kind of utopia lost. What Marx and Thoreau shared with Jesus was a sense that "the letter killeth." It was not the letter as Mosaic Law that killed but as secular "legality." Legality had so saturated the human world that it stood before it as a kind of second nature. But it was a false nature that brought not life but death. And yet we take this world up as our own, as if it were our duty to do so.

The opening pages of Thoreau's *Walden* are devoted to describing the failed ethic of the world into which he was born. "The greater part of what my neighbors call good I believe in my soul to be bad, and if I repent of anything, it is very likely to be my good behavior. What demon possessed me that I have behaved so well" (12). The primary good of which Thoreau repented was the virtue of work. In work we do what is not good. The world of discipline in work is, for Thoreau, a morally inverted world. It is human nature standing on its head. It is what Thoreau sought to convert. Again like Marx, Thoreau saw much of the horror of work in the way it incorporated the human into the machine.

> I see young men, my townsmen, whose misfortune is to have inherited farms, houses, barns, cattle, and farming tools; for these are more easily acquired than got rid of. . . . Why should they begin digging their graves as soon as they are born? . . . But men labor under a mistake. The better part of the man is soon plowed into the soil for compost. (8)

This is perhaps not a view of the grim English factory that Marx had in mind, but it is enough to allow Thoreau to say, "But lo! Men have become the tools of their tools" (30), and "he has no time to be anything but a machine" (9).[7]

Thoreau's analysis of what it is that compels men to work is no less acute: money and the ruin of human time. It is the money-form, as Marx called it, that has captured and distorted a more human notion of time. Time, for *Homo economicus*, is not the river I fish in. It is for exchange. We trade our time for money. Our houses themselves become, in time, mere potential for exchange, or accumulated "equity," as our bankers tell us. The true cost of a thing, Thoreau shrewdly observes, condensing hundreds of pages of Marxist analysis to an epigram, is "the amount of what I call life which is required to be exchanged for it, immediately or in the long run" (25–26). Money does not fool Thoreau. Money always wears the face of the boss. It represents the loss of freedom and ultimately the loss of self. One is not human in the unequal world of work for exchange. One is compost in the making.

All of this makes what we actually do with money tragic (and stupid). We sacrifice our lives so that we can buy "shoestrings." Most of the things we buy are not only not necessities but hindrances. Instead of considering what a house is, how it serves us, and learning how to make one, we shut ourselves in a "suburban box."[8] Our home becomes a part of death: "The spirit having departed out of the tenant, it is of a piece with constructing his own coffin—the architecture of the grave—and 'carpenter' is but another name for 'coffin-maker'" (37).

Mass these coffins together in neighborhoods, and we soon come to resent our neighbors as if they were to blame for our shared cemetery, our "whitewashed tombs." What we might not see so clearly is that "the bad neighborhood to be avoided is our own scurvy selves" (27). Consider the vinyl-clad subdivision nearest you. No argument is needed to complete this thought, although it's worth observing that, as Thoreau wrote, the people who live in these subdivisions "appear never to have considered what a house is" (29).

Similar though Marx and Thoreau may be in their account of the consequences of living in a society defined by money, their suggestions for how to respond to it are poles apart. Forget the Party. Forget the revolution. Forget the general strike. Forget the proletariat as an abstracted class of human interest. Thoreau's revolution begins not with discovering comrades to be yoked together in solidarity; it begins with the embrace of solitude. "I never found the companion that was so companionable as solitude" (95). For Thoreau, Marx's first and fatal error was the creation of the aggregate identity of the proletariat. Error was substituted for error. The anonymity and futility of the worker were replaced by the anonymity and futility of the revolutionary. A revolution conducted by people who have only a group identity can only replace one monolith of power with another, one misery with another. It perpetuates the cycle of domination and oppression. As Nietzsche put it, "It would be extraordinarily dangerous to believe that humanity as a *whole* would continue to grow and become stronger while the individuals become flabby, equal, average . . . humanity is an abstraction" (quoted in Morgan, 200). And: "Now people are trying to conceive *the flock as an individual* and ascribe a higher rank to it than to the individual—deepest misunderstanding!!!" (quoted in Morgan, 123). For Thoreau, too, it is in solitude that the individual becomes most human, which is to say most spiritual, and in a sense most *revolutionary*.[9]

Having first taken the famous step of stripping his life of the extraneous, reducing it to "simplicity, simplicity, simplicity" and committing himself to solitude, Thoreau reveals that his real purpose is "ethereal." "It appeared to me that for a like reason men remain in their present low and primitive condition; but if they should feel the influence of the spring of springs arousing them, they would of necessity rise to a higher and more ethereal life" (33). This ethereal realm is not the result of any familiar or formal religious practice. The ethereal is gained by simply doing one thing, consciously. "I made no haste in my work, but rather made the most of it." What is divine is simply being attentive to what you are doing in the moment you are doing it, assuming that that thing is not merely stupid (i.e., anything you have to do to receive money) or reflective of a life that is "frittered away by detail" (a good description of a country of double- and triple-taskers, driving a car, while talking on a cell phone, the local classic rock station wailing through the Bose speakers, while wiping the baby's nose, with the classifieds on your lap, all the while thinking of where you'll eat for dinner). Thoreau recommends simply being "awake" to what is in front of you. As one of his "rude" country visitors to Walden put it, "Maybe the man you hoe with is inclined to race; then, by gory, your mind must be there; you think of weeds" (104).

Instead of emptying oneself out into work (virtue), routinized work hollows out the worker from the inside (debasement).

As a spiritual and poetic economics deeply unlike Marx's "political economy," Thoreau's thinking emphasizes drift. As he puts it, his life required a "wide margin" for drifting, for trusting to an intuition of what comes next. (The happiness of the drifter would later be called "joyful wisdom" by Nietzsche: the union of "singer, knight, and free spirit" through whom conventional morality is "freely trodden on.") If one objects that drifting does not allow for a national economy of millions of people, Thoreau's answer is probably that the very idea of a nation is a bad idea. A State is a "desperate odd-fellow society" made up of "dirty institutions" (118). There is no nation that one can join in good conscience, not while it sells humans "like cattle, at the door of its senate-house" (118). If we wish to reduce the exploitation that is the essence of money, then we need less money, not more. A national culture based on the universalizing of money and ever more possessions is ultimately, as we say now, "unsustainable." Which is a euphemistic way of saying that it is a culture bent on making provision for its own death. We are always busily providing for our own defeat.

Thoreau's idea of civil disobedience is embedded in the counter-Enlightenment of romanticism, transcendentalism, and the Imagination, and it is, like Jesus's revolution, an appeal for Life over Death. How right the antiabortionists are to urge us to "choose life," but how wrong they are to imagine that the culture of death is limited to abortion. Our entire disposition toward each other and toward Being, that supreme "given" that we call the world of nature, is a disposition to death.

Thoreau was the first to recognize the spiritual, intellectual, and economic tendency of America toward a culture of death, but he was also the first to begin to think about the hopefulness of re-claiming life. For Thoreau, the most basic question to ask of the vil-lage (as he did of tiny Concord) is what kind of human beings it produces. His answer was not optimistic. "We are a race of tit-men, and soar but little higher in our intellectual flights than the columns of the daily paper" (77). The ethical health of Concord had nothing to do with the presence of a glowing sign that reads "Glory to God in the highest" or the din of "testifying" that the evangeli-cals insisted upon, and it did not have to do with material prosper-ity. For Thoreau, it had only to do with a spiritual presence about which one cannot speak at all! "What is religion?" Thoreau asked in his journal (August 18, 1858). "That which is never spoken." But when this spirit and its silent persuasion are missing, the community is capable of great and violent stupidity. Then what, Thoreau would ask, does it mean to say that in our community young people are asked to grow up into the following: you will abandon your private intelligence in the name of public stupidity (patriotism, in particular) in order to do something as dubious as learning to kill other humans? And yet this is what passes as virtue in our own time and what passed for virtue in Thoreau's. As George Santayana wrote, "Why practice folly heroically and call it duty? Because conscience bids. And why does conscience bid that? *Because society and empire require it.*" Put more spiritually, as Simone Weil does, "Evil when we are in its power is not felt as evil but as a necessity, or even a duty" (*Gravity*, 71).

Thoreau's advice to us is simply "don't join it," this society of duty, this empire of legality.

3.

A quote in Ralph Waldo Emerson's *Representative Men* begins to capture my sense of what is necessary to confront our culture of duty and legality: "What is best written or done by genius in the world, was no man's work, but came by wide social labor, when a thousand wrought like one, *sharing the same impulse*" (quoted in Matthiessen, 134, my emphasis).

So, the question we might ask of the future is, When will we again share the same impulse? Now, this might sound like a merely self-absorbed wondering after and waiting for the next zeitgeist, the next Age, the return of the sixties counterculture. It will certainly disappoint the more practical and ideological on the left. But I would contend that what is needed is not simply the overthrowing of the present corrupt system in the name of an alternative political machinery that will provide something like "authentic participatory democracy." The appeal of this familiar leftist position is that it can tell you what needs to be done *now*. Overthrow state power. But I think that part of our reluctance to share this particular revolutionary impulse is that we remember the little Lenins and their big ideas, and we remember where these guys led us: group gropes on the Weatherman bus as a prelude to bombing a post office. Or, worse than that, endless boring meetings with the next "progressive" Democratic candidate who is going to "turn this country around" and "return it to the people." Right. All you really need to ask the John Kerrys or Howard Deans of the world is where they stand on free market trade issues. They're all ultimately for it, the whole complex scheme of World Banks, NAFTA, WTO, and so forth. And they're for it out of a sense of duty to "national interest," "jobs for working people," or whatever other shameful thing it is that they use to paper over violence. The rest—corporatism, militarism, environmental disaster, human disaster—follows automatically. Saying "The world must keep its ports open" really does imply "The bombs must keep falling for now" (not to mention the "peaceful" continuation of the economic exploitation of vulnerable populations both here and abroad). They say it doesn't mean that, but it does.

So, where should we look if we can't look to the self-styled revolutionaries and the establishment progressives? Thoreau's suggestion should still be ours: a return to the fundamentals of being human.

The Imagination has always called for a return to the truest Fundamentalism contained in the question "What does it mean to be a human being?" Needless to say, this is a question that deserves the deepest and most patient development. It will have to suffice for the present to say that our reigning social reality forbids—structurally, politically, violently—the broad posing of this question. If we could pose the question and Thoreau were allowed to answer, his answer would imply at least three things: First, a refusal of the world as it stands. Second, a recommitment to fundamentals. What does it mean for a human being to need a house? Food? Clothing? Is the prefabricated suburban box a human home? (Ruskin called these fundamentals "valuable material things," and his list is strikingly similar to Thoreau's: land and house; food and clothing; books and works of art. These are the things that Marx classified as possessing "use value" as opposed to money's exploitive "exchange value.") Third, an understanding that to stand before the question of these fundamentals requires spirit. Thoreau called it awareness. I make my home with *this* plank. I make my food with *this* seed. This awareness is really simply a form of prayer, and our culture is nearly bereft of it. As Simone Weil—perhaps the strangest and most unlikely Thoreauvian solitary, outcast, and transcendentalist of all—wrote, echoing Thoreau's sense of "awareness," "The authentic and pure values—truth, beauty, goodness—in the activity of a human being are the result of one and the same act, a certain application of the full attention to the object" (*Gravity*, 120). Or, more tersely yet: "Absolutely unmixed attention is prayer" (*Gravity*, 117).[10] It is perhaps the saddest, most hopeless thing we can say about our culture that it is a culture of distraction. *Attention deficit* is a cultural disorder, a debasement of spirit, before it is an ailment in our children to be treated with Ritalin.

When we can meet again, as the revivalists say, and share an impulse that separates us from a state not only distracted but apparently bent on its own destruction, and when we can again confront work in a way that reconnects us spiritually with human "fundamentals," then we will have recalled life from the culture of death.

That is Thoreau's meaning.

Anything short of that, I'm sorry to say, seems to me in one way or another simply to acknowledge that we're not fishing attentively at the side of the river; we're caught in the current, and the current is going to take us where it's going to take us: no place pleasant and certainly no place very just.

Clearly, what I am calling the Spirit of Disobedience is not a blueprint for revolution. It is first, and most usefully in the present, the recognition that the idiotic either/or theater of American political reality is itself a problem because it prohibits us from thinking through the real problems and their possible solutions. (Christian/

humanist, Republican/Democrat, conservative/liberal: stupid!)
But the Spirit of Disobedience is also, ideally, the actions of a lot of
people who are first individuals "sharing an impulse" and acting
with a determined independence to refuse the present and assert a
version of the next world. The agent of this assertion will be, in
Slavoj Žižek's telling phrase describing Jesus's original community,
"a collection of outcasts" (123). The Spirit of Disobedience is the expression of the desire for the next Turning of the Age, even if that
age never comes. When we love something intensely in spite of the
fact that it not only doesn't exist, but we don't know what we mean
by this thing—justice, freedom, God itself—that love is the expression of a desire for it to become real, to become our reality. As Žižek
writes with tremendous power, "As every true Christian knows,
love is the *work* of love—the hard and arduous work of repeated
'uncoupling' in which, again and again, we have to disengage ourselves from the inertia that constrains us to identify with the particular order we were born into" (129).

This may all sound hopelessly abstract and impractical and
utopian. Oddly, it's just the opposite because there are so many examples of this "spirit of disobedience" at work. More than anything, it is the expression of a loyalty to life. Its practitioners are a
sort of secret current of American spirit, completely outside (if not
repulsed by) the sort of orgy of self-love that we witness in parades
on Memorial Day and the Fourth of July.

Let me give you an example, briefly, with which I am familiar.
In 1951, a group of American Quakers, fleeing the military draft,
moved to the central mountains of Costa Rica in order to establish
a community. They bought large tracts of land, farmed about 10
percent of it, and left the remainder of the forest in its ancient, virgin condition in order to protect the watershed and preserve the
natural beauty of the area. In 1972, the Monteverde Cloud Forest
Preserve was established, and it now protects 10,500 hectares of
cloud forest, biological diversity, and, to put it simply, hope for the
maintenance of something like "the Good." The resplendent quetzal,
a magnificent bird, has a viable home here. The quetzal is evidence
of a certain kind of grace, and if that seems obscure to you, simply

consider the fate of the quetzal in neighboring Guatemala, where it is the "national bird" and yet nearly extinct in that part of its range in spite of the honor. (The Guatemalan quetzal mirrors the fate of our own animal icons—the eagle, the buffalo, the mountain lion, the wolf, and the bear—whose presence among us is suffered only with the greatest anxiety as our industries and subdivisions take over ever more of their habitats. It is then that we see what our real values are.)

We need many, many more Monteverdes, forests that are not merely for banking natural resources for future pillage, as in our so-called wildlife and forest preserves that preserve nothing that a stroke of the congressional pen can't annihilate. Monteverde is an expression of energy moving between religious faith, human caring, and a sense of belonging to the natural world. The Quaker sense that consciousness, or the Inner Light, *is* the presence of God in the world, and that the world standing before that light is real and commands our reverence, leads them to reject the false Real of the empire of legality and the "shock and awe" of ultimately self-defeating violence that maintains it. Monteverde is the enduring consequence of disobedient people sharing a spiritual intuition and creating a desirable human future in a flourishing natural world. But in recent years even Monteverde has been threatened by what is happening in much of the rest of the planet, threatened especially by globalization and climate change. The famous *sapo dorado*, or golden frog, has not been seen in Monteverde's cloud forest in over a decade and may be extinct, a victim of a pollution that penetrates even to the cloud forest. And ominously the news arrives from Brazil: yet another highway—a $417 million project to turn BR163 into a two-lane tollway stretching 1,100 miles—is to be built through the Amazon for the convenience of soybean kings and at the mortal risk of everything that merely seeks to *live* there.[11]

Simone Weil describes the human condition as a balance between gravity and grace. Unhappily, in the present, gravity—the ethos of capitalist materialism—far outweighs the effects of grace, the counterpressure of spirit. We cannot change that fact through an act of mass political will. The Leninist fantasy is dead. But we will have an opportunity to reassert "grace," and it is not far off.

Here's why: industrial capitalism as we have known it for the last two hundred years is the consequence of an economy built on the onetime availability of cheap oil; but, as James Howard Kunstler makes unmistakably clear in his recent book *The Long Emergency: Surviving the Converging Catastrophes of the Twenty-first Century*, the exhaustion of cheap and readily available oil is probably no more than two decades away. (The depletion of copper, essential for communications and computing, is said to be no more than fifty years away.) If cars don't work, the suburbs don't work; if the suburbs don't work, Wal-Mart doesn't work; and if Wal-Mart doesn't work . . . what's left in our splendid suburban service economy? Roger Bentley, formerly of Imperial Oil in Canada, and Roger Booth, who spent his professional life at Shell, believe that when the oil peak hits, "A crash of 1929 proportions is not improbable." Colin Campbell, the founder of the Association for the Study of Peak Oil (ASPO), puts it even more bleakly:

> The perception of looming decline may be worse than the decline itself. There will be panic. The market overreacts to even small imbalances. Prices are set to soar in the absence of spare capacity until demand is cut by recessions. We will enter a volatile epoch of price shocks and recessions in increasingly vicious circles. A stock-market crash is inevitable.[12]

We should recall that the social instability of the last global depression bred not only poverty and suffering but also social opportunity. Socialist thought flourished, stimulating the federal government to the greatest project in social justice legislation in our history, the New Deal. Unhappily, the moment also produced fascism. How many of us, desperate to maintain the "American lifestyle" of the last fifty years, will be willing to vote for violence as a way of maintaining that lifestyle, even if it means the loss of fundamental liberties? (Our quiescence in the face of recent federal wiretapping revelations already answers this question to a degree.)

If we don't want a fascist future, we'd better be prepared with an alternative.

As the "unsustainability" (as we euphemistically call it) of an oil economy comes closer and closer to fully revealing itself as what it has always been—a culture of death—and our economy begins to sink into the carbon bog from which it first rose, there may be worldwide misery and social chaos, but there will also be an opportunity, but only if we are prepared for it. Individual efforts at the Good will have this opportunity to *socialize their impulses* and effect an increasingly consequential counterbalance to the logic of global capitalism. The automobile, suburb, strip mall not only will not be welcome in this moment but will simply not be possible. Industrial agriculture will finally be revealed as the bad idea it has always been: a pipe dream of tasteless and nutrient-deprived "plenty" utterly dependent on the availability of fossil fuels and petrochemicals. As we look at the wreckage left to us by a century and a half of extravagant greed and waste, we will be able to ask, as Thoreau did, "What does it mean to be a human being? What are my fundamentals?"

Although the sixties counterculture has been much maligned and discredited, it attempted to provide what we still desperately need: a spirited culture of refusal, a counterlife to the reigning corporate culture of death. We don't need to return to that counterculture, but we do need to take up its challenge again. If the work we do produces mostly bad, ugly, and destructive things, those things in turn will tend to recreate us in their image. (This is particularly poignant with relation to the awful food we eat and the plague of obesity we are presently suffering. We eat piles of fatty food and become diabetic blimps as a consequence.) So, we need to turn to good, useful, and beautiful work. We need to ask, as Thoreau and Ruskin did, "What are the life-giving things?" Such important questions are answered for us in the present by the corporate state while we are left with the most trivial decisions: what programs to watch on TV and what model car to buy.

Reclaiming the right to ask the serious questions is no doubt an invitation to utopian thinking, with all the good and bad that form of thought has always implied. But what utopian thinkers have understood best is that if utopia is "nowhere," *so is everywhere else.* "Reality," whether defined by evangelical Christians or empiricists, is a form of disenchantment (it's "nowhere, man," as Maynard G. Krebs put it). The Real, on the other hand, is up for grabs. What the earliest utopians—Montaigne, Thomas More, Tomasso Campanella—understood was that they fought not for a place but for a new set of ideas through which to recognize what would count as Real. Equality, not hierarchical authority. Individual dignity, not slavish subservience. Our preeminent problem is that we recognize the Real in what is most deadly: a culture of duty to legalities that are finally cruel and destructive. We need to work inventively—as Jesus did, as Thoreau did—in the spirit of disobedience for the purpose of refusing the social order into which we happen to have been born and putting in its place a culture of life-giving things. In such a society, not only could we claim to be Christians, but we'd actually act like Christians.

So let the age turn, as St. Paul promised. We're well done with this world. And let that new world finally begin.

Chapter 5

A New Fundamentalism:
Time, Home, and Food

Let me begin this last chapter with a controversial thesis. There is not now nor has there ever been anything united about the United States of America. We are not one. The idea of a unified American character is not so much a myth as a bad joke that won't go away.

I advance this brutal fact in the way that an alcoholic family will advance the brutal fact of the alcoholic's addiction. We are not a "happy family." We are in pain. No healing of the family can take place without this acknowledgment, and no happy resolution to our national traumas can take place without first addressing certain delusions about who we are. In spite of what should be obvious in our history, the idea of a unified American character is a pious assumption for everyone from William Bennett (on the right) to Ken Burns and even Michael Moore (on the left), all of whom are as willing as the most disingenuous politician to speak of the "American people" as if we all knew what that meant. But this sentimental appeal to a united America is becoming increasingly difficult to maintain with a straight face. The nasty and very public fighting of our eternal "culture wars" has placed our differences in high and belligerent contrast.

It may be that the only united thing about us is the dicey thing called mass consciousness. Mass consciousness is the creature of a million disparate sound bytes, polls, think-tank analyses, patriotic

Hollywood palaver, and lugubrious presentations by news anchors. It is a reservoir of unexamined assumptions about who we are that functions as a sort of second nature. In truth, it can claim "unity" only because it is so utterly artificial. It is, after all, this massed consciousness that decides to go to war. It is this massed consciousness, a creature of endless polls and dubious elections, that gives its assent, provides its mandate, and thus legitimacy to the next exercise of national might. Massed consciousness can say only yes or no. It is a thing of neither faith nor reason. It is thinking as perceived by number crunching. It is the kind of social authority first created in Andrew Jackson's triumph through the majority rule of the mob: "King Numbers." It is what Alexis de Tocqueville called "the great and imposing image of the people at large." It is nothing and it is everything. Meanwhile, the human beings among us, the sentient individuals, of which there are fortunately still more than a few, are desperately saying, "Yes, but . . . ." Yes, protect us from terrorists, *but* stop doing the things we've done to create the terrorists in the first place, *but* don't create more terrorists in the process, *but* don't eliminate our liberties while you're at it, *but* don't behave like terrorists to protect us from terror. Feed us, *but* don't destroy family farms and local economies, *but* don't poison the environment, *but* don't destroy the world's fisheries, *but* don't turn the countryside into a giant factory. It is all of these *buts*—the endless qualifications, reservations, objections, and hostilities—that are finally oppressed. Mass consciousness is what ordinary people think, or so we're told even though no one has yet produced an ordinary person. As for your *buts*, take them up with your priest or your therapist.

Worse yet, when politicians express a desire for a return to shared values, a united America, what they are really saying is that the other side should die and go away, especially that little far-flung army of individuals with their infinite *buts*. For instance, the day after his 2004 election victory, President Bush said that he wanted to heal the divisions in the country and that he would reach out to all Americans. But at the press conference two days after his election, he said that he had amassed political capital and was going to spend it and that he would reach out to "everyone who shares our goals." This sort of reaching out screams, "Go away!" Clearly, at such moments we are not far from a confession of what de Tocqueville called the "tyranny of the majority." For the George Bushes of the world, democracy is, as the joke goes, five wolves and four sheep deciding on what to have for lunch.

What no one seems to want to imagine is that our divisions are not going away because they are our most enduring national trait. What no one seems to want to imagine is that the basics of national identity have not changed in 250 years. Our culture war is not about current affairs; it is a fundamental *enmity* in our national character. For us, civil war is the norm, not a sad episode in our distant past. We are still either freethinking Deists or evangelicals. We are still either Thomas Paine, Enlightenment rationalist, or John Wesley, the father of populist, evangelical Methodism. Now and again, these two sides have found reason to endure consensus as we did during the Revolutionary War (or, more humbly, as we all do when we have a particularly odious conservative/liberal in-law over for holiday dinner). But by and large culture war is a *founding* reality of American life. And it is not going away.

What the counterculture of individuals, this nation of "but-sayers," would like to propose—if mass consciousness would lay off the high-decibel yammering for a moment so that something other than its own voice could be heard—is what I would call a New Fundamentalism. The world that money creates, as we know too well, is the world of the condo, the subdivision, the mall, and the interstate that takes us to the next condo/subdivision/mall complex. It is the world as conceived—quite rationally, I might add—for the convenience of corporations. This "convenience" is greater than any other consideration in the world. (For example, not even the risk of incurring the wrath of Aztec deities could stop yet another Wal-Mart megabox going into Teotihuacán, Mexico. Now from the Pyramid of the Sun you see the world as imagined by Sam Walton.)

Contrary to the habits of capitalist world making, the New Fundamentalism desires to immerse us in the remaking of the human world. This alternative human world may not have the effect of uniting our forever divided national culture, but it can ideally serve as a call to people of whatever background to consider what it is that is most common to us. The difficulty is that few of us know how to say no to the present, we don't know how to "disobey," and we don't know how to provide a different future than that planned by corporate capitalism. If we're concerned about the kind of human future we are creating, we must also be concerned with how we are living in the present. Unhappily, how we live is presently the near exclusive concern of corporations and media conglomerates which have, together, turned every Main Street into the same street and made the inside of every American head echo with the same vacuous music and movie/TV scenarios. This is the arena in which a spiritualized disobedience means most. It doesn't mean a second New Deal, another massive bureaucratic attack on our problems. It doesn't mean taking to the streets, throwing bricks through the window at the Bank of America, or driving a tractor through the local McDonald's. It means living differently. It means taking responsibility for the character of the human world. That's a real confrontation with the problem of value. In short, refusal of the present is a return to what Thoreau and Ruskin called "human fundamentals, valuable things," and it is a movement into the future. This movement into the future is also a powerful expression of that most human spiritual emotion, Hope.

In the sections that follow, I have the privilege of talking with three people who are heroically engaged in the creation of a New Fundamentalism of human things. I will speak with John de Graaf about Time, with James Howard Kunstler about Home, and with Michael Ableman about Food.

1.

John de Graaf is the national coordinator of Take Back Your Time Day, an annual event scheduled for October 24 (see www.timeday.org) and a frequent speaker on issues of overwork and overconsumption in America. He is the coauthor of the best-selling *Affluenza: The All-Consuming Epidemic* (2001). He is the editor of *Take Back Your Time* (2003) and of the children's book *David Brower: Friend of the Earth* (1992).

De Graaf has worked with KCTS-TV, the Seattle PBS affiliate, for twenty-three years, as an independent producer of television documentaries. More than fifteen of his programs have been broadcast in prime time nationally on PBS. He is also the recipient of more than one hundred regional, national, and international awards for filmmaking. He produced the popular PBS specials *Running Out of Time*, an examination of overwork and time pressure in America, and *Affluenza*, a humorous critique of American consumerism. His other national PBS specials include *For Earth's Sake: The Life and Times of David Brower; Visible Target; A Personal Matter: Gordon Hirabayashi vs. the United States; Beyond Organic; Escape from Affluenza;* and *It's Up to Us: The Giraffe Project and Circle of Plenty.* He recently completed two new documentary films, *Silent Killer: The Unfinished Campaign against Hunger* and *Buyer, Be Fair: The Promise of Product Certification.*

Prior to his work in TV, de Graaf was public affairs director for KUMD Radio in Duluth, Minnesota. He has taught documentary film production at the University of Washington and the Evergreen State College. He is the founder of the Hazel Wolf Environmental Film Festival and former president of the Hazel Wolf Environmental Film Network. He is the recipient of the Founders of a New Northwest Award for his work in environmental media. He is also the co-chair of the Public Policy Committee for the Simplicity Forum, a national think tank for the Voluntary Simplicity movement.

CW: I've been trying to think through a politics of refusal that assumes an "outside" to dominant assumptions about American politics and culture. It's clear to me that somehow you found yourself on the outside arguing against what just about the entirety of the political spectrum considers "reasonable." Can you provide a short autobiographical sketch of how you discovered yourself so much outside of "received political wisdom"? Were there major influences of an intellectual or practical nature for you?

125

JD: There have been many influences. The first was a childhood spent backpacking in the Sierra Nevada (often only with friends, sometimes even alone by the age of fifteen). I learned the value of solitude and an appreciation of the natural world and formulated my own thinking about what was important. But I am not a solitary person, and my personal experience tells me that sharing the wonder of the world with others is key—to my happiness, at least. I appreciate people and city life and human connection. Like my hero, David Brower—the Thoreau/Muir of twentieth-century America—I like wilderness as "dessert."

Nonetheless, my experiences with wilderness helped shape an independent spirit I think. Beyond this, my views were shaped by my experience with poverty as a VISTA volunteer on an Indian reservation from 1965 to 1967. I gained a passion for justice, but I also learned that stuff doesn't create happiness when I taught on the Navajo reservation in 1969 and saw that kids who had nothing were far more creative—they never talked about being bored—than my ten-year-old brother and his friends, whose rooms looked like Toys 'R' Us stores and who always claimed they had nothing to do.

It was always clear to me that I wanted to control my time—I didn't want to be trapped. I didn't want to have to give up those weeks of backpacking in the mountains—though now I seldom do it anymore since I have overfilled my own schedule. My love for the environment meant that so-called quality of life politics always appealed more to me than traditional left politics. I came to understand that our environment could not survive unlimited growth—so that materialism was not only not the route to happiness; it would pave the way to biosphere collapse if left unchecked. I came to understand this even better while producing *Affluenza*.

My intellectual thinking was shaped especially by the young Marx, whose analysis of alienation and whose emphasis on the centrality of free time—"the realm of freedom"—seemed totally true to me. Beyond that, I was powerfully influenced by both Fromm and Marcuse—whose Frankfurt School Marxism chal-

126

lenged the material growth paradigm. Ivan Illich was the thinker whose "outside the box" analysis really persuaded me. He made it clear that the unlimited market is not only environmentally unsustainable but that it destroys the capacity of people to create a world together. His book *Tools for Conviviality* just made so much sense.

On the other hand, I've felt it important to be politically practical and to try to reach people where they are and not where I want them to be. I felt the anti–Vietnam War movement, in which I was very active, was hugely out of touch with average Americans. Moreover, trips to Cuba convinced me that the so-called socialist countries were no model for the industrial West—they were far too restrictive of human freedom. So while I don't think of the northern European social democracies as Utopia, they seem at this point in history to produce by the far the best *results*—more justice, somewhat less consumerism, stronger protections for the environment, nonbelligerent foreign policies, the right to choose time over money and quality of life over quantity of things. I see my personal historical mission as at least to try to help move America in that direction.

CW: Why "time" as the place where you hunkered down for the long fight?

JD: Because no one else was really addressing what I feel is the central issue. Marx knew that true wealth is "disposable time, and nothing else." If we are to become sustainable, we cannot grow on without limits. Our American ecological footprint already would require five planets if the entire world were to adopt our lifestyle. We simply must begin to trade increases in productivity for time instead of stuff—there is no way around this. But I believe that this is not a sacrifice. The sacrifice is what we are doing now. Americans are sacrificing health, families, communities, the environment, their true spiritual needs, and their own happiness as they work longer and longer to compete for a materialistic dream that does not make them happier and undercuts all the other values they claim to hold dear. I also believe

this issue has resonance beyond left and right. Really, what makes Europe different is that they have, to a much greater degree, chosen time rather than money as the reward for their productivity. I think this issue gets right at the heart of what makes Americans so depressed and stressed out as a society. I also believe this issue is winnable if people begin to understand it. And I am optimistic that this is starting to happen. Check out what Ralph Nader wrote about the strategy meeting Take Back Your Time just held in D.C. with leaders of many organizations and a number of congressional staff:
www.commondreams.org/views06/0109-.

CW: So what led to the creation of the Take Back Your Time organization?

JD: The Simplicity Forum, of which I am co-chair of the public policy committee, was looking for public policy ideas that might help lead to a more simplicity-friendly society. We all agreed that trading productivity for time instead of stuff could help create a more sustainable environment and offer people a positive alternative to materialism. We didn't believe that exhortations to sacrifice for the sake of the planet were working and that we needed to show folks that they are already sacrificing one of the most important forms of wealth they have—their time—for the sake of things that don't make them happier and deplete the Earth. The result is that they are stressed, lonely, and hurting in many other ways. We believed we needed a hook to get this message out, and we remembered that the first Earth Day led to the passage of all the most significant environmental legislation in U.S. history—all within three years of the first Earth Day and all signed by a conservative Republican president, Richard Nixon. We thought, "If Earth Day could do that, maybe a Time Day could create similar awareness of time poverty." We chose October 24 as the date because it was a Friday (in 2003, the first year) nine weeks before the end of the year, symbolizing the nine weeks more that Americans are on the job each year compared with

Western Europeans. Serendipitously, it also turned out that October 24 was the anniversary of the day in 1940 when the U.S. got the forty-hour workweek. That's it, essentially.

CW: What are your most concrete aspirations as a group? How realistic do you think they are?

JD: We had hoped that Take Back Your Time Day would be like Earth Day. That wasn't very realistic, but the movement has received enormous media attention and I think that slowly our message is getting out there. We have now established a Time to Care coalition to try to put public policies like paid family leave, sick leave, vacation time, benefits for part-timers, limits on overtime, et cetera, on the political agenda. We are optimistic that some key political figures will raise these issues in the 2006 elections. We just had a major meeting at the AFL-CIO in D.C. with many groups and several key congressional staff to develop our 2006 public policy campaign, and I am optimistic that it will have an impact, though it's too early to tell how large it will be. We'd like to make time poverty a household word or, rather, phrase, that helps explain to people what is happening to them.

Our biggest problem is that we have had to do everything on a shoestring. With one exception, we have not been on the radar screen for foundations—the time issue is not on their screens—so we have accomplished all we have done on about $15,000 a year. All my work has been volunteer, for example. We cannot continue to be viable unless that changes. So, I am cautiously optimistic, but I realize we have a huge mountain ahead of us.

CW: Don't you think that one of the main obstacles to legislation freeing our time is that the values of the Boss have been internalized by workers?

JD: In a word, yes. It's quite amazing, really. Though there are signs that many people recognize the problem and that workers would choose more time away from work, even, in many cases, if they earned less. And we hear from many, many people who really feel this. The problem is that they also feel hopeless that they can change it. That to me is the greater obstacle. There is a huge sense of resignation out there.

CW: Let me give you one concrete example. One of the routines of public life here in Illinois are letters to the editor or to political representatives complaining that (1) professors don't work and (2) their "research time" is a boondoggle fleecing taxpayers. In my work with the Illinois Board of Higher Education, I've tried to reverse the question: why aren't we demanding time for creativity from the business world for all workers? In some ways, it's almost as if the populist complaints against universities is a version of "misery loves company": "If I have no freedom, why should I pay for yours?"

JD: Too true. But this is the natural symptom of a society which has been continually exhorted to look out for number one, et cetera. There is generally no sense of the common good or that it might be sensible to pay for some things, like health care and family leave, through taxes instead of paying much more later in excessive market charges. We have been persuaded that we are number one as a country and that everyone wants to be like us, when every UN quality-of-life statistic I examine puts the U.S. near the bottom among industrial countries. We somehow have to challenge that blindness but do it in a way that seems patriotic and pro-American. It's a daunting challenge.

CW: How do you start to get the people who have most to gain on your side?

JD: We hope that we'll reach them through new messaging about the issue that starts with loss of family time, focuses on people's having "earned" time off through all their hard work, emphasizes that "we have responsibilities" like families, community, environmental stewardship, personal health, and that we need time for outside the workplace. I find that the ecological footprint works for many people to see that our current lifestyle is not sustainable. We need to show comparisons with other countries.

Ralph Nader suggests that we put out pamphlets that say, "Did you know that Wal-Mart gives twenty days of paid vacation to their employees the first year on the job? Oh, sorry, that's Wal-Mart in Germany." Humor is very important, and we try hard to avoid being strident. We are working on the issue from many directions—speaking, teaching classes, forming coalitions, creating briefing materials for candidates, working to get political leaders to address the issue—and from many angles—debt and bankruptcy, materialistic children, health and obesity, family breakup, loneliness, trashing of the environment, the teaching of our prominent faiths, et cetera. We need to try many things—there is no one way to start. We are new at this, just getting our feet wet, but learning rapidly, I think.

CW: When I was doing radio interviews for *The Middle Mind*, one of the things that I heard with surprising frequency was "That's all well and good. I'm sure you're right. But I have a job! It's all I can do to work eight hours a day and get my car home without dying on the freeway. I don't have time to do something about the Imagination." I was essentially being told to get a clue. At last, though, it occurred to me that if people don't feel they can be active participants in their own culture and active shapers of their own lives, they're oppressed. People can be oppressed because they're physically repressed, or they can be oppressed because they have had so much of their waking life and energy taken from them that the end result is the same. Do you think that this is at some level a strategy? Is it sensible to imagine that at some level the "ruling class" (for want of a better term) thinks, "We won't educate people that we don't need as workers because we don't want educated people hanging around with nothing to do. And we don't give time to the people we do have to educate because, again, you don't want educated people with the time to think about the world they live in"? Is it something like that?

JD: I don't know, really. I'm sure there are people who think of it that way, but I really can't imagine a grand conspiracy.

131

CW: Is it just good old primitive creation of profit for capitalists? "Crack that whip. I'll tell you when you can go home."

JD: That's my hunch. The owners of capital want to get as much as they can for their investments as quickly as possible and at as low a cost as possible. When benefits like health care are a big part of the compensation package, it makes more sense to work existing employees as long as possible instead of hiring new ones. In this country, we have several factors that lead to requiring longer work hours from people: Health care is employer provided; pensions, except Social Security, are employer provided; there is no legislation except the Fair Labor Standards Act limiting hours; and it has been progressively weakened as more people are now called "managers."

There is no legislated vacation time, paid family leave, paid sick leave, and so forth, as exists in nearly every other industrial country. Unions are weaker than ever and tend to fight for money rather than time. High personal debt levels encourage people to seek overtime and trade time for money, rather than vice versa. Business has all the political power now, with no countervailing leverage for workers.

CW: Is it possibly also just an ingrained stupidity of the American Protestant work ethic?

JD: I don't think it's the work ethic as much as it is the power of business. In the 1930s to 1960s, the U.S. was a leader in achieving shorter work hours. Things really changed in the mid-1970s when the conservatives' political strategy captured government. In 1974, *Business Week* editorialized, "It will be a hard pill for most Americans to swallow: the idea of having less so that business can have more. Nothing that this nation has ever done can match the selling job required to get the people to accept the new reality." But accept it they did and the result is that the U.S. has dropped vis-à-vis other industrial countries in virtually every measurement of quality of life—from health to equality to trust to education to you name it—except GDP per capita, ever more unequally distributed.

132

It's mostly the economic effect of unbridled capitalism. I'm not anticapitalist; I'm a social democrat. I believe the Scandinavian model, while far from perfect, provides the best balance between what the market can do well and what must be done through government. But time poverty is also the result of our inner poverty, needing to fill every moment with distractions or toys and leading us to use every labor-saving gain to produce more rather than to be and to appreciate the natural world, each other, and so on. Of course, these two causes reinforce each other.

CW: I think it was St. Augustine who described two orders of human time. One is *chronos*, the arrow of time, one damned thing after another. This notion of time we Americans get almost too well. But we seem to live in it as if we were people who didn't know they were going to die. The second order of human time Augustine calls *kairos*. That is a sort of time out of time. Sacred time. Time in which we transcend chronos. Is there a spiritual dimension to time that you or your organization are interested in?

JD: Absolutely, which is why I mention the inner poverty that leads us to fill every moment. And why we need to fight for sacred time—the Sabbath or its secular equivalents, whatever they may be. It's why we are working to reduce the overscheduling of children and to encourage "four windows of time" when people just enjoy each other without doing or spending. It's why we encourage the conscious trading of money for time. We are working with the Massachusetts Council of Churches on these things. In some ways, time poverty will not change until we as a people begin to value other things, but it's a dialectical process. When people win more free time as in Europe, they actually find that they enjoy social time in the cafés, or traveling by bicycle, or walking in nature rather than expensive amusements, and they want even more free time as a result. This is the irony: Americans, who have the least free time, are the least concerned about having it because they don't experience the joy it can bring. So we have a lot of educating to do.

CW: My last question is simply "Is there an answer to a question that you've always wanted to give but never had the opportunity because no one asked the question?"

JD: Your last question is a great one, but I think the answer is no because I just sort of stick in what I want to say regardless of the question—I enjoy bending the rules. I'm not deep enough a thinker to think of things people wouldn't think to ask me, I think.

2.

James Howard Kunstler was born and raised in New York City, except for a three-year hiatus (1954–1957) in the Long Island suburbs. He went to a remote, minor branch of the SUNY system, worked as a newspaper reporter, and ended his corporate career as an editor with *Rolling Stone*. Since 1976, he has been writing books—nine novels, including *Maggie Darling*, *The Halloween Ball*, and *An Embarrassment of Riches*—and a series of nonfiction books on the fiasco of suburbia—*The Geography of Nowhere*, *Home from Nowhere*, and *The City in Mind*. His latest book, *The Long Emergency*, is about the global energy predicament and its ramifications. Since 1976, Kunstler has lived in Saratoga Springs, New York, a classic "main street" town halfway between New York City and Montreal.

CW: As a social critic, you are outside not only the mainstream but any stream that I know of. No one else calls the United States a "national automobile slum." Can you provide me with some autobiographical details on how you discovered yourself so much on the "outside"? What were some of your most important influences, both practical and intellectual?

JHK: I am not the best judge of where my point of view fits on the spectrum of opinion, except I would like to think I go my own way.

In politics, I suppose I am officially a registered Democrat, but the ideas that my homies have developed over several decades are odious and absurd to me—everything from the cant of multiculturalism (i.e., opposition to common culture), to the politicization of personal gender identity problems, to (most particularly) the ethos of despotic intolerance that characterizes political correctness. All these (and more) are inventions of the hippie generation, which I was part of, and I regard them as intellectually disgraceful in the plainest sense of the word.

On the other hand, the idiocy of so-called conservatism and its alliance with the agents of superstition and ignorance (Christian fundamentalism) are equally repellent to me. There does not seem to be any refuge for someone with common sense at the moment.

By the way, there are a great many people with common sense still out there, and I am sure they are extremely disaffected by the current situation. But I also understand that societies periodically get lost in the wilderness, so to speak, and this is such a time for American intellectuals. This failure of ideas, incidentally, is preventing us from squarely facing the great problems of our time.

My influences? I was a poor student. I loathed high school. My college board scores would have put me in the "moron" category. I became a theater major at the third-rate state college I attended because amateur show biz was easier than English lit or differential calculus. I graduated straight into "Grub Street" journalism, freelancing for the hippie newspapers of Boston and Cambridge in the early 1970s. The atmosphere there was evolving early PC, and so naturally I did not fit in, though I managed to get a lot of colorful stories published. These clips eventually got me a job on a legit daily newspaper where I was mercifully left alone to write more colorful features. Then I made the mistake of taking a "glamour" job at *Rolling Stone* magazine, which was a miserable experience. After that, I dropped out to write books.

The only "mentor" I ever had was the guy who taught directing for the stage at my college, a rather brilliant young fellow named David Hamilton, who got me reading Samuel Beckett. At the time, I had found on my own such literary stylists as Tom McGuane, H. L. Mencken, Robert Brustein, Van Wyck Brooks, and Bernard Devoto (all of them now more or less forgotten figures).

I educated myself writing my own books. The nonfiction I began turning out in the 1990s, especially, required a lot of searching in the thickets of history and philosophy to turn up ideas that would allow me to construct a coherent worldview. Coherence counts for a lot, especially in an incoherent culture.

CW: How did you decide that "Home," how we live, how we organize our communities, would be a major focus for your work?

JHK: I was disgusted with the everyday environment that had evolved in my lifetime, especially suburbia, and the concurrent dereliction of our cities and towns. It seemed to me to present the most disturbing symptoms of an extremely troubled society, and I set out to investigate it. Everything I looked into along these lines corroborated my sense that we were committing collective suicide by constructing a living arrangement with no future. It was extremely serious business.

CW: One of the many things that I find fascinating about your work is the way your social criticism is inflected by your novelist's nose for drama. It is unique for someone looking at housing and urban planning to have as a major conclusion that that landscape is "tragic." And you provide such insightful examples of just how this tragedy unfolds as when, in *City in Mind*, you stitch together three commercials and a news report to reveal an increasingly typical American drama: debt, failure to manage debt, bankruptcy, and crime/prison. A sociologist would simply display a statistic, like the fact that there were more bankruptcies than college graduates in these early years of the twenty-first century (a powerful statistic in itself). But you look at the same thing and see story and tragedy. Can you comment on your own movement from novelist to social critic? Why not just have your novels carry this work? In the past, of course, the novel was the most important tool of social criticism, as with Dickens, Hugo, Orwell, Conrad, and others. Is the novel finished as an instrument of social change?

JHK: Well, my friend and colleague Andres Duany likes to say that we are suffering from a plague of overspecialization. There are not enough generalists on board, he says. In America, there has been tremendous competition in the various fields to establish scientific cred—especially in the training grounds for these things, academia—and the result is an extreme and inordinate infatuation with statistical analysis. In short, we've created a smorgasbord of pseudosciences which, finally, do not really inform us very well and, most of all, fail to add up to a coherent view of anything. These days, for instance, I get indignant letters all the time from various alternative fuel mavens citing reams of statistics about the "efficient" production of ethanol or some other rescue remedy for our car-dependent way of life, and their figures are all very impressive—until you realize that all this "study" is in the service of promoting a living arrangement that sucks out loud anyway. I hate these motherfuckers.

I never made any transition from novelist to social critic. I was functioning as a social critic in my twenties writing for newspapers. My novels are full of discourses on society. Of course, I was writing them in precisely the era when the novel was losing its preeminence in our literature (and the reviewers generally ignored them, anyway). I turned back to journalism (the "Nowhere" books) after I'd burned out writing novels. (I'd published eight of them, and I was waiting on tables at night.) I needed a break, a change of focus. By then, I had enough experience in the world and developed enough of a writing style to attack these themes in a fresh way.

Few people were addressing the issues of the everyday environment. There was barely any context for labeling it as a subject. Some people called it "landscape studies," which was barely adequate, in my opinion. Jane Jacobs and Lewis Mumford had made powerful statements on cities and suburbs back in the early 1960s, but the subject demanded an updating by 1990. Tony Hiss really started the ball rolling with his 1989 book *The Experience of Place*, but he really only struck a glancing blow on the subject. The academics writing about urban design were totally fucking hopeless, boring, and mostly *wrong* in their conclusions. Leon Krier was developing an eloquent polemic, but he was over in Europe, and he did not favor the long form. Mostly he put out epigrams and diagrams.

I had been writing some stories for the *New York Times Magazine* about land development in America and the problems it entailed. After three or four of them, I pitched a story with the working title "Why Is America So Fucking Ugly?" and they gave me the green light to write it up. Once I did, they rejected it. The *Times Magazine* always rejected anything with either wit or an interesting point of view—and if you happened to slip one in on them, the editorial board always found some way to extract every single joke from the piece. I hated those cocksuckers. They were like a literary politburo. Smug, supercilious, fretful little bureaucratic douche bags. They didn't have enough soul to be actuaries. And even if you made it through the grueling editorial wringer and got your story—with all the heart and soul wrung out of it—into print, then they'd jerk you off for months about cutting the paycheck. I wanted to go down to 43rd Street with a fungo bat and beat their fucking heads in. But instead I took that rejected manuscript about "Why Is America So Fucking Ugly?" and turned it into a book proposal, which my agent wound up selling to one of the more high-toned imprints of Simon and Schuster. That was published as *The Geography of Nowhere*.

CW: I grew up, in the 1950s, in the suburbs of San Francisco, in a "vet village" called San Lorenzo. It was one of the first pre-fab communities in the United States where the assumption was that the working people would have to leave the community to find employment. Its nickname was actually "Levittown West." Every morning, my father would walk to the bus stop and make a long commute to the business district of San Francisco. He called San Lorenzo a "white ghetto." But your opposition to suburbs is not only practical, in terms of their unsustainable dependence on cheap oil; you also are clearly opposed to them on aesthetic grounds. Being a sensitive son of the suburbs myself, I know well why you might hate the mass conformity of the California suburbs where jigsaw butterflies on the garage door make do for beauty. But what do you do about the ugliness and kitsch of the suburbs at this point? Critics like you and me are often accused of elitism because we are disdainful of the idea that people might actually like their vinyl-clad horrors. Mass kitsch consciousness seems nearly as imponderable and insuperable as the domination of corporate life. What has to happen at the level of consciousness to allow the manmade environments of the United States to become beautiful again?

JHK: The destiny of the suburbs would seem to be tracing a tragic path. They were built in haste without love or care, strictly as mass-produced commodities for profit. They are entering a period of severe disutility. And they lend themselves very poorly for retrofitting into something better and more useful. In my opinion, they will simply lose value and become the slums of the future—before eventually becoming the ruins of the future. And they will not be picturesque, either. They will only last long enough to mock us for tragically misinvesting all our twentieth-century wealth in a living arrangement with no future.

As we enter the new post–fossil fuel era of hardship, there will be little patience for kitsch and its derivative ironic poses. After all, kitsch is the fake appreciation of awful artifacts for the boldness of their awfulness. Only a superaffluent society lacking in a real sense of purpose can invest psychic energy in this kind of decadent aesthetic.

It seems self-evident to me that life in the years ahead will necessarily be more local and that the artifacts we produce will be more locally made and less the product of machine mass production. A return to human scale (from the high-speed car scale) will inevitably prompt us to pay more attention to fine detail. The outside of buildings will matter again. We are likely to be restricted to regional materials in a menu of things found in nature. We will be subject to fewer diminishing returns of technology, which is what the ugliness of everyday America is largely about today. In fact, I think it can be stated with some precision that the immersive ugliness of our time is entropy made visible.

CW: One of my favorite things to do each summer is watch the Tour de France on TV. But I don't watch entirely for the competition. I'm fascinated by the lovely little towns that the tour runs through. They're diverse in architecture without being incongruent. They're mostly reddish-brown and made of brick or stone. The streets are narrow and winding and more inviting to pedestrians and, of course, bicycles than to cars. Somehow, they still seem to have a sound economic base although it's hard to see where the industry is. People seem comfortable on the street, sitting in cafés and sipping their espressos. It just looks so human. There is very little sign of any franchised commerce. But in the United States, similar small towns are economically devastated. They're in wretched repair. They look like ghost towns. Economic vitality rarely means much more than whether or not they can keep the corner franchise convenience store open, and even these are increasingly in gas stations, which means that the center of small-town economic and civic life is a gas station. About the only places that have preserved a sense of the traditional American community (outside Disneyland) are tourist towns. It's almost as if the traditional American community has become a sort of museum. But there is still no economic core other than what the tourists themselves provide at restaurants and gift shops. In short, we take vacations to the places where we ought to be living. What kind of cruel irony is that? And just what do the small towns of rural France know that we don't? Why are they not victims to the same forces that we are victims to?

JHK: In the late twentieth century, Europeans made some different choices about their living arrangements than Americans did.

Europeans have always had a scarcity relationship with petroleum. Except for a little oil patch in Romania, which was contested in both world wars, and the North Sea bonanza, which is now firmly in depletion, Europe had no oil of its own. So, notwithstanding the horrendous disruptions of the twentieth century, Europe never embarked on quite the same sort of drive-in utopia that America did. They built some suburbs and super-highways, but they did not concurrently destroy their cities and their small towns.

Our oil industry was the world's first at the truly continental scale. We had plenty of our own oil and a poor understanding of its ultimate limits. So we let her rip. We destroyed our cities remorselessly, because building the alternative universe of the car-dependent suburbs was so profitable, and driving was fun! Gasoline was extremely cheap here for most of the twentieth century.

Since American cities and towns were mostly products of the industrial age—and all the unpleasantness entailed by it—we never had a high regard for cities in the first place, or for city life. There is no Renaissance Cleveland. No Medieval Kansas City—and thus very little residue of a non-machine-made, human-scaled urban environment. Then there is our whole mythologized romance with wilderness and rural landscapes, which came to be viewed as the antidote to the horror of city life—and was then delivered to the public on a commercial basis in the form of suburbs.

When, after World War I, we got around to imposing an overlay of automobile infrastructure on top of our industrial cities, which were already pretty repulsive places, there was nothing left to feel any affection for. And Americans reacted accordingly. Eventually, we continued the process of destruction in our small towns, too. Because the scale of our small towns was necessarily smaller and more human than our industrial cities, we retain a more conscious sense of loss associated with their destruction. But this sentimentality was no match for the profit motive. We destroyed our towns anyway for the benefit of the car dealers and the homebuilders. In the process, of course, we also destroyed a great deal of agricultural landscape, with ramifications that will become apparent to us later in the twenty-first century. Then we gave ourselves a consolation prize—Walt Disney World.

We also allowed giant predatory corporations to destroy all the fine-spun local networks of economic interdependency that kept our towns alive. Bargain shopping was not such a great bargain after all. With no local commercial class left, there were no caretakers left in our towns.

To be succinct about it: Europe preserved what it could of its central cities and small towns and the life associated with them. Europe retained robust public transit at all scales: heavy rail, light rail, et cetera. Europe had different land tenancy and development regulations, more heavily weighted toward the public interest than ours in America. Europe did not destroy local agriculture. In fact, much to the annoyance of other nations (and even among themselves), Europe subsidized local agriculture and the small-scale, value-added activities associated with it (e.g., cheese, winemaking, etc.). To some extent, these activities have sustained the economies of the French small-town scene. However, the economies of these towns have been greatly assisted by tourism and by foreigners purchasing vacation villas in them. This is apt to change in an energy-scarce future when there is much less mass tourism and people are unable to travel as freely as they are currently able to. For instance, the commercial aviation industry, as we have known it, may cease to exist altogether a quarter-century from now.

This has been an extremely prolix answer, and I apologize for that, even though I probably left a lot out (that is why one writes books). But I would add a final note. The choices we made in America were tragic choices. Our aggregate suburbias can be described as the greatest misallocation of resources in the history of the world. We threw away all our twentieth-century wealth on an infrastructure for daily living with no future. We didn't have to do this, but we did, out of sheer greed and stupidity. We will now suffer the consequences.

CW: One of the powerful suggestions of your analysis of urban and suburban life is simply *walking*. It's almost as if your prescription for correcting the things that are wrong with the way we live is simply "walk" and the rest takes care of itself over time (a recommendation as simple and difficult as Zen's encouragement to "just breathe"). Can you comment on that idea?

JHK: It is self-evident to anyone who visits a town or city designed on the preautomobile basis. It is all about scale. When the streets and buildings are scaled to the speed of walking, then any journey through them can be deeply rewarding. All the details of design resolve into legibility. The retail presents itself in the form of shop windows that can be enjoyed. The buildings present details—columns, scrolls, swags, patterns, reliefs, and so forth—that represent conscious efforts to create beauty and meaning. Even the handwriting on the chalkboard outside the bistro is done with care. That's Paris, or Rome, or a hundred other urban places in Europe.

Compare that to Chicago, where I was last weekend. I walked from the Art Institute at Michigan Avenue, west on Adams Street, clear across the Loop to my hotel on Madison out by the Dan Ryan Expressway, about a mile. Most of the fine-grained urban fabric of prewar Chicago buildings has now been replaced by sets of gigantic despotic skyscrapers hiked up over parking structures or that simply present blank walls to the street (and to the pedestrians there). Sometimes you get an air-conditioning vent instead of a blank masonry wall. Whoopdedoo. Once in a while, you'll come across a shop front—a Starbucks chain café—but blankness is the overwhelming theme on these streets. Why did Chicagoans allow this to happen? Well, despite the retention of the old street grid, the city has pretty much surrendered to the automobile. The streets were made one-way, and parallel parking is not allowed on the sides—which tends to increase the speeds of the cars (the streets actually perform like minifreeways.) The result is deeply unrewarding for someone not in a car.

Much of New York City operates a lot better in this respect, even Manhattan, where the vertical scale is the same as Chicago—that is, despite the presence of skyscrapers. For instance, you can walk down Fifth Avenue in Midtown Manhattan and where the buildings meet the street the retail is exactly the same small scale that you would find in Paris, and the prewar buildings (even the skyscrapers) offer details at the street level that are consciously designed to be beautiful—the sculptural transoms at Rockefeller Center, for instance. But go over one block to 6th Avenue (renamed Avenue of the Americas in the 1960s), and it's Chicago all over again: blank walls, no action at street level from the buildings, no shop fronts. Just meaningless windswept plaza setbacks mandated by 1960s zoning laws in a misguided attempt to force the developers to provide "open space"—which turned out to be meaningless and represented a complete misunderstanding of urbanism per se.

The bottom line is that our urban design culture reached a state of utter collapse in America by the late twentieth century. We had forgotten just about every useful principle or method for assembling a place worth being in. Now it happens that the New Urbanist movement heroically came along in the 1990s and dove into the Dumpster of history and retrieved a lot of that principle and methodology. But the public is still not ready to use it again—they just want to stay in their fucking cars—end of story. And the officialdom of municipal planning and their colleagues in the departments of transportation are all still defending the methods of the postwar era.

That will all change drastically and quickly as the global energy crunch gains traction. But here in America we will be left with the job of reforming and retrofitting practically everything, and we will be a far less affluent society, without the means to do much.

One final thing. Some hidden villains in this story are the senior citizens who form the majorities on most of the planning boards across America—because they have time on their hands and are able to devote themselves to public service. These old farts have lived through the entire extravaganza of the automobile age. Not only is the capitulation to motoring absolutely normal to them, but they have especially benefited from it in their elder years as living in an environment designed mainly for cars is easier for them than having to walk a few blocks for anything. Hence, this gerontocracy has done everything possible to sustain the dominion of the car in millions of insidious decisions made by local planning boards all over America. To make matters worse, it seems rude, even uncivil, to oppose such generous, public-spirited folks. But the evil they do needs to be revealed.

CW: You talk about the "failure of the critical faculties" in this country. One of the things that perplexes me about social activism is that both the structures of authority *and* the public seem to resent intelligence. I serve on a faculty advisory body to the Illinois Board of Higher Education, and we have been told by state bureaucrats, politicians, administrators, the general public, *and our own faculty members* that if we want our advice to be welcome, it should be unfailingly sunny in outlook and that we should not be "arrogant" (by which they mean we should not claim to know anything; we shouldn't act like "experts"). I have to say that I am dumbfounded by this attitude. Why would anyone want their best-educated people to hide what they know? Your work is not so much negative as disdainful. For me, you earn every bit of your disdain because you are so patient in showing why public and economic policy is shortsighted and ultimately doomed. But isn't this a sort of catch-22 for critics? If we're critical and intelligent, we're resented and rejected. I mean, John Q. Public actively goes out of his way to express his *hatred* for the intellectuals. But if we try to accommodate conventional thinking (which way too many of my colleagues do), we're irrelevant. Are social critics doomed to be Cassandras? Believed only when it's too late to do anything about it?

JHK: I think what we are seeing vis-à-vis authority in our society these days involves something more fundamental—the loss of legitimacy. Authority without legitimacy is no authority at all. This authority also goes to laughable extremes to defend itself, since it is not grounded in legitimacy.

This is visible in an interesting way right now in the disposition of our political parties. The Democrats and Republicans have become, respectively, the Mommy Party and the Daddy Party. At the actual household level, of course, both Mommy and Daddy across the nation have uniformly lost legitimacy and authority where child rearing is concerned—hence the thuggish behavior of children in all social ranks, from the ghetto to the prep schools, and the inability of parents to control them.

At the political level the Republicans have managed to discredit the idea of male authority by miserably mismanaging our economy, our energy predicament, and our foreign relations. The Democrats have discredited themselves by resorting to kindergarten gestalt therapy as the sovereign remedy for all political ills (what has come to be seen as political correctness).

The public, of course, are not passive victims of these conditions, but active participants. They have subscribed to sets of bad ideas in both parties and they are suffering the consequences.

For example, the Mommy Party wants everybody to get along at all costs—including the cost of a common culture that would afford orders of unity to a diverse nation. So they affect to celebrate diversity—minus the one thing that would permit diversity to really work, the unity of a common culture, common standards of behavior, agreed-upon standards of excellence, et cetera. They are thus able to enjoy getting brownie points for having good intentions, without having to endure any of the difficulties of exercising real social rigor (or making tough choices, or taking a stand that some things really are better than other things).

Wherever this misrule reigns we find disaster, particularly education, and in universities especially where, in my lifetime, women have hijacked the humanities departments and turned them into gestalt therapy workshops or grievance committees. At its worst, for example, you see sick behavior (as reported in the *New York Times* last spring) at Brown University, where counseling staff helped twenty-year-old girls get their breasts amputated to support the validity of their gender identity crises. (We'll skip over the self-hatred implicit among the Mommies here.)

The Daddy Party, on the other hand, in its desperate pursuit of authority-at-all-costs, makes alliance with the agents of superstition and ignorance—the born-again Christians—who are simply hung up on sex, when all is said and done. The Daddy Party has misplayed just about every other matter of importance pertaining to our national survival: in promoting the destructive suburban sprawl economy; in selling out America's productive capacity for the swindle of "globalism"; in surrendering standards in banking, lending, and credit creation; and in ruinous military adventuring. In sum, the Daddy Party has cast aside any sense of true broad responsibility—the fundamental acceptance of the fact that our actions have consequences. Instead, Daddy just promises a series of "treats"—tax cuts, hydrogen cars, space voyages—and makes false promises—like the idea that our currency will retain its value or that we will become "energy independent" without changing our living arrangements.

So it's no wonder that authority has lost legitimacy.

However, politics, like nature, abhors a vacuum. When things get bad enough, something else will rush in to fill that vacuum.

My own pet theory is that Americans have been so lax, so complacent, passive, self-satisfied, feckless, and foolish, that the time will come (soon, probably) when they will beg to be pushed around by real authorities. They will beg for leaders who tell them what to do or forcibly direct them into purposeful activities (for the purpose of saving their own asses). That's the true fascist threat, not pathetic little George W. Bush.

Now, to get to the final part of your question. I am often chided by lecture audience members who accuse me of failing to offer "positive solutions" or remedies to the problems I present. This is fucking nonsense, of course. I lay out a comprehensive view of restructuring all our vital everyday activities—agriculture, commerce, schooling, urban design—the message being that there *is* an intelligent response to the problems I lump together as "The Long Emergency." But characters like these audience members don't want to hear that. It's too fucking difficult. They'd have to change the way they're living now. All they want is a different liquid fuel to pour into their gas tank so they can keep cruising for burgers. There is no help for such feckless slobs.

CW: I read an advertisement in the *New York Times* yesterday [March 1, 2006] assuring the world that there was going to be plenty of oil in the future. I almost cried. Not because I think they're wrong but because I *hope to hell* they're wrong. Why should we be relieved to think that there will be an endless supply of the thing that is killing us? It's sort of like our attitude toward jobs: we hate them but are terrified that we're going to lose them. I really hope to live long enough to see what happens in the aftermath of cheap oil. But as you have remarked, how that time will break is uncertain. Violent, *Mad Max*–type anarchy and violence? Or a desirable return to the local? What's your optimum hope?

JHK: I am more interested in imagining likely outcomes than hoping and wishing.

You can state categorically that delusional thinking rises in tandem with economic distress, so we should expect a more incoherent public discussion, not a better one. You mention that Exxon-Mobil ad in the *New York Times*. Well, that was in response to a piece that ran only in the *Times* online edition earlier that week, by Robert B. Semple Jr., stating that Peak Oil was for real, and we'd better start behaving accordingly. The chicken-shit *Times* editor kept it out of the print edition, for reasons unknown.

Politically, I think the American public has been so feckless, complacent, self-satisfied, and passive that, as we find ourselves in rising hardship, the public will beg for politicians who will push them around—or, more precisely, direct them to purposeful activities aimed at saving the country's collective ass.

That could conceivably be a better outcome than just sinking into a Hobbesian swamp of desperate individual (or tribal) self-defense. Or it could be worse. The Germans tried it in the 1930s, and it didn't work out so well.

But I worry also that we may exhaust and bankrupt ourselves attempting to defend the "entitlements" of our drive-in utopia. Suburbia is going to fail whether we like it or not, but we've invested so much in it that we will probably do everything possible to prop it up. It will prove to be a tremendous exercise in futility if we do.

CW: When you try to think about these problems of community in spiritual terms, what do you come up with? Is the return to a local community and a local economy also a return to a certain lost spirituality for you?

JHK: I'm writing a post–oil age novel now as an exercise in imagining these very things. I do think that Wendell Berry got it right when he wrote about the disastrous results of us "selling our allegiances" to corporations and distant oligarchies. Getting away from that would certainly present opportunities for a true revival of community life. Anyway, so many of the perceived boons and benefits to our current way of life are attended by huge diminishing returns, which we have totally ignored. For one stark example, the increase in private suburban luxury has been at the expense of meaningful public life. So you can wallow in all the splendor of your home theater and enjoy relationships with fictional characters on a screen, but you will sacrifice the company of real people and real relationships in the process. One of the reasons that the Oscars is such a compelling event for the public is that they imagine having more significant relationships with movie stars than with people who live on their street.

From a more explicit angle—and writing as someone totally uninvolved with organized religion—I think that the church in all its forms could come back much closer to the center of American life, and I don't mean just the born-again yahoo variety, either. I mean real mainstream participation in mainstream organized spiritual practice. All our other authorities may be in a state of deep discredit, loss of legitimacy, and eclipse and the public will be desperate for some organizing agency in their collective lives.

Even "sophisticates" will participate, whether they believe strictly in some deity or not. The church may also be the only structure able to organize schooling in the years ahead, or the two activities may be blended together.

Science, on the other hand, may end up being demonized. It will partly deserve it, but we will lose a lot in the process.

3.

According to *Sierra*, the magazine of the Sierra Club, "Michael Ableman is a gracious rebel who knows that industrialized farming wrings the life out of both soil and communities. His joy in stewardship and in people celebrates a psychic sustainability that won't appear on spreadsheets."

He is the founder and executive director of the Center for Urban Agriculture at Fairview Gardens, a nonprofit organization based on one of the oldest and most diverse organic farms in Southern California, where he farmed from 1981 to 2001. The farm has become an important community and education center and a national model for small-scale and urban agriculture, hosting as many as five thousand people per year for tours, classes, festivals, and apprenticeships. Under Ableman's leadership, the farm was saved from development and preserved under one of the earliest and most unique active agricultural conservation easements of its type in the country.

Ableman has started food gardens at the Santa Barbara AIDS Hospice, an eleven-acre farm at the Midland School, and a market garden at the Jordan Downs housing project in Watts. Working with low-income communities from L.A. and New York City to organizations as diverse as the Esalen Institute and the International Association of Culinary Professionals, Ableman's work as an educator and consultant has helped to inspire numerous projects and initiatives throughout North America.

In 1984, Ableman traveled to mainland China, where he observed the remnants of a traditional system of agriculture that had sustained people and the land for thousands of years. This experience inspired him to travel around the world documenting other cultures, culminating in the internationally acclaimed publication of *From the Good Earth: A Celebration of Growing Food around the World* (1993). Called "hopeful and inspiring" by the *Los Angeles Times* and "a compelling photographic essay" by the *New York Times, From the Good Earth* was one of the first books to visually document the dramatic changes taking place in food and agriculture worldwide. The book has become a timeless classic that challenges us to participate in the marketplace, in our kitchens, and in our own backyards.

Ableman's second book, *On Good Land: The Autobiography of an Urban Farm* (1998), is the emblematic story of his fight to preserve a piece of what was once some of the richest farmland in the world, and a paean to the sweet obsession of growing food. The *Philadelphia Inquirer* stated that "if Henry David Thoreau had been a farmer, he would have written a book very much like Michael Ableman's *On Good Land." Booklist* called it "inspiring and utterly absorbing" and the literary book review *Kirkus Reviews* said that "among a sprawl of books incessantly issued and hyped, this small, wise volume quietly calls us to read and be renewed." The book, graced with Ableman's lush photographs, argues articulately for farmland preservation and provides a blueprint for a farm that thrives in cooperation with its surrounding community.

He has lectured extensively throughout the United States and in Europe. His work has been featured in *National Geographic*, the *Utne Reader*, and *Gourmet*; on National Public Radio's "All Things Considered"; and twice in front-page coverage in the *Los Angeles Times*. An award-winning film about Ableman's work, *Beyond Organic*, narrated by Meryl Streep, aired nationally on PBS in 2001.

His third book, *Fields of Plenty: A Farmer's Journey in Search of Real Food and the People Who Grow It*, was released with an accompanying PBS film in 2006.

Ableman lives and farms on an island in British Columbia with his wife and two sons.

CW: I want to say before I start these questions how beautiful and inspiring I found your books, especially your new book *Fields of Plenty*. They really had on me the effect I'm hoping this book will have on people: make them want to live differently. You've opened up the human and social problems of food for me in a way that makes it clear that simply buying from the organic corner of the local megachain supermarket is not anything close to an answer to these problems.

I feel strange about this first question because of the photographs in your first book of Fairview Gardens, your famous "urban farm." They show this tiny green area absolutely surrounded by, dissolved in, digested by the Southern California sprawl around it. Talk about the belly of the beast. And yet I need to ask, what was your personal journey to the "outside," to convictions and a vision not only of agriculture but of human life so at odds with the assumptions of the industrialized present?

MA: I left home when I was seventeen. I had a burning need to get beyond the books and talk and peer pressures of high school and get on with my life. But when I got out and took a good look around, when I considered how I might fit into the world and what work I might do to survive, I realized many livelihoods, while providing an income, were sucking the life out of the world. I was deeply troubled by this, and after a short stint studying photography, I dropped out and joined an agrarian-based commune.

Growing food seemed to be one of the few livelihoods, when done thoughtfully, that could actually contribute to the health and well-being of the world rather than taking from it. It also seemed to be one of the few professions I could pursue that supported my contrary nature and my need for independence.

The commune I joined had three different parcels of land totaling some four thousand acres on which we raised row crops, orchards, operated a complete goat and cow dairy, and produced grain and fiber. We supplied our own natural food stores and bakery and juice factory and restaurant as well as feeding ourselves. We even made our own clothing, backpacks, and shoes.

After only four months living in that community, I was given the responsibility of managing the one-hundred-acre pear and apple orchard located in a high desert valley east of Ojai, California. At the time this was one of just a handful of commercial orchards in the country that was farmed organically. Here I was at the age of eighteen with no orcharding experience, having never managed anything, directing a crew of thirty people, most of whom were older than I.

The orchard had been abandoned for fifteen years, and the branches between trees had become so intertwined that you couldn't find the alleys down the middles of the rows.

All I had was a 1930s copy of *Modern Fruit Science*, the journal from the guy who ran the place the year before and gave up in frustration, and a copy of Goethe's famous quote "Whatever you can do or dream you can, begin it. Boldness has genius, power and magic in it," which I attached to the door of my twenty-foot unheated trailer.

Now this could have ended up really bad, and under most similar situations, I would have probably spent the rest of my life working in a high-rise office building. But there was something that took place down those rows of apple and pear trees, something very different than what is happening in most agricultural fields and orchards in North America.

I went to work each day with thirty of my friends, and while we worked, we joked and talked, and we discussed our dreams. We tried out our latest theories and philosophies on each other, speculated on the fate of the Earth, and ate our lunch together under the shade of the trees. In the winter we pruned every day for four months straight, in the spring we thinned fruit, and in the fall it was a ten-week harvest marathon.

It was repetitive work, but at the end of each day, instead of feeling like I had been chained to some mind-numbing drudgery, I felt like I had attended an all-day party. The work got done, the orchard thrived, and those apples and pears gained a reputation around the country. And while the cold nights and hot days of that high desert provided ideal growing conditions, I am sure that the fruit was equally infused with the energy of that group of people and the pleasure they found in each other and in that land.

This was my introduction to agriculture. This community experience has informed all of my agricultural endeavors since; it demonstrated that good food is more than just the confluence of technique and fertile soil, and that it is the result of men and women who love their land, and who bring passion to working with it.

Leaving the security of the commune brought me face to face with a very different reality. Agrarianism was definitely not where the world was going, and while I got an amazing education during those five years in the commune, the experience made it all too clear that I was pursuing a profession that most folks saw as a form of drudgery, something to get away from. And yet I had come to see it as one of the most life-giving, creative, artistic, nurturing, delicious things that I could possibly do.

I ended up working a small farm, an island floating in a sea of tract homes and shopping centers located in Southern California for over twenty years. During the early years working that farm, I witnessed the remaining rich agricultural land around us disappearing at a rapid rate, replaced by tract home developments. As new suburban neighbors moved in, I found myself fighting for the farm's right to be. I was threatened with jail time over our compost piles and over the crow of the roosters. I had a choice: hole up and fight this alien force that surrounded us, or build bridges, provide an invitation for folks to learn and get involved, work to educate the new urban neighborhood that now surrounded us. I chose the latter and turned the farm into one of the earliest and most successful working farm/education centers in the country.

Our biggest challenge came when the land itself was under threat. We had one year to raise almost $1 million to save the farm from development. In eight months we did so, placing the land under one of the first active agricultural conservation easements in the country, a document attached to the title of the land that gives that land a voice, requires that it continue as an organic farm and education center, and protects it in perpetuity.

As the project and staff grew, I became more administrator than farmer, and I eventually decided I needed to get back to farming. So my family and I moved to a farm we purchased in British Columbia (land in California was too expensive) and started over again. We thought we had found our little piece of paradise, but duality exists everywhere. We soon discovered that the pulp and paper mill on neighboring Vancouver Island was planning to begin burning tires, railroad ties, and coal in one of their power boilers and that we were essentially living across the street from what was to become a toxic waste incinerator. Once again I found myself unintentionally forced into having to stand up, organize, and protect. We organized a clean-air concert with Neil Young and friends, and raised huge amounts of money to both research and fight the multinational corporation that operated the mill and eventually stopped the proposed burning. But in the process I received hate mail, even threats. More importantly, I discovered that there is nowhere to go, there is no paradise but the internal one, and that learning to see is a dangerous thing—it demands participation and action.

CW: Were there important intellectual influences for you?

MA: My greatest influence has been the land that I work. Anyone who believes that farming is boring or monotonous or not incredibly creative should consider that it is one of the few professions that allows one to work every day within an amazing ever-changing biological system. The most important agricultural skill is not operating a tractor or soil science or propagation; it's observation. Every moment I am on my land, I have the opportunity to witness the continual unfolding of nature's drama. Learning to really see deeply into that drama is a skill that I bring to so many other aspects of life as well. I'm not a big reader, and as a writer I don't normally read material that is on a topic similar to the one I write about (afraid of regurgitating), so my influences are less intellectual and more experiential, observational, social, and cultural through the people that I meet and work with.

CW: One of the things that I find fascinating and unexpected about the interviews that I've done for this book is that although I thought that I was going to be interviewing social activists with very practical concerns about how we live, I discovered that all of you have primary self-identifications as artists. John de Graaf is a filmmaker, James Howard Kunstler is a novelist, and you are a visual artist. I myself am a fiction writer. And so the approach to social issues as they have developed in these conversations has been strongly aesthetic. It's as if we start with a part—time, home, food—but thinking through the part seems to require a vision of the whole. Your interest in food is an interest in the world but more importantly the world made beautiful. That really is beyond organic. Can you comment on the role of the beautiful in your work?

MA: I came to farming more as an artist than an agriculturalist. I was concerned about this at first, worried that my emphasis on the visual and the beautiful might get in the way of the production aspects of farming. I have since discovered that the instincts of the artist are very important when applied to agriculture. Sadly, most people, including many farmers, view farms as "production units," food factories, forgetting that many of the most successful farms have been established based directly on observations of nature. Natural systems are always beautiful to look at; nature has always provided the deepest inspiration for all of the arts. I have found that there is a strong correlation between the visual strengths of a place and its productivity. In my latest book, *Fields of Plenty*, I return to the theme of the relationship between art and agriculture many times throughout the book.

I often find that people are surprised or even bewildered when they discover that a farmer can also write or make photographs or play music. It's the stereotype image in their brains of a farmer as slightly stupid, dressed in overalls, with a pitchfork in his or her hands. When you consider that farming is one of the few professions in which the practitioner is out on the land every day observing nature, it's hardly a surprise that many farmers are inspired writers, musicians, and visual artists.

I sometimes feel that good farming is the greatest form of artistic expression. Farmers create the bridge between nature and human nourishment. Food as the product of the agricultural arts goes beyond any image on the wall of a gallery or museum. Good eating, in that sense, could be considered one of the most integrated forms of art appreciation.

CW: Back in the day, I'd go to the food co-op in Berkeley for granola and other hippie comestibles. That was a truly grassroots, countercultural affair. But now the mainstreaming of organic means that affluent and almost exclusively white Americans drive their Saabs to Wild Oats and then pick up a latte at Starbucks. Of course, there are still small local whole foods markets and farmers' markets, but the future seems to be with franchise operations and, once again, economies of size. How does alternative food production get to the point where it's something more than a niche for the affluent, where it is a central concern for what it means to have a whole and healthy human community regardless of income?

MA: I cannot tell you how many times I give a speech, and during the Q&A some good-intentioned person asks, "So, Mr. Organic Farmer, why aren't you and the rest of your kind doing more to feed the poor?" The simple answer is that the problems of a social and economic system that has created haves and have-nots is not just the problem of farmers (many of whom are struggling themselves to survive). Ultimately, access to pure food is not an agricultural problem; it is a social problem and should be shared by the society as a whole. (I also get the question "How is your proposed system of agriculture going to feed growing populations?" Same thing: population is a social and cultural problem, not an agricultural one. There is no agricultural system that will be able to feed the kind of population growth we are seeing in some parts of the world.)

It is true that most of the "organic" food that I have produced over the years has only been available to a narrow percentage of the population—those who could afford it. We had to survive. With that said, many farmers like myself have been very creative in developing projects to get our food and the knowledge to grow it into lower-income communities. There is a very strong "community food security" movement in the country (primarily run by nonfarmers).

Beyond that, "cheap" food is only cheap at the supermarket. We often end up paying for it many times after we've left the checkout counter. "Cheap" requires that it be grown with an arsenal of chemicals to control "weeds," pests, and to feed crops that are now growing in soil so depleted that it has merely become a lifeless medium to hold the plants up in the air. There is enough evidence now that that arsenal of chemistry is a significant contributor to a number of chronic and even epidemic health problems, including cancer. American agriculture is now totally dependent on people from Mexico and points south to do the work in the fields that Americans will no longer do. As a nation, the U.S. guards the borders to keep out the very people whose hands harvest the food that we eat. "Cheap" food is dependent on cheap labor and folks who often live and work in conditions that are marginal at best. "Cheap" food is cheap because we pay for it in our taxes. Approximately $46 million a day in subsidies go to the landlords of large-scale industrial farms and not to farmers. And the hidden cost of "cheap" food is a host of environmental degradations: the nation's top soil eroding and disappearing at a staggering rate, freshwater aquifers pumped beyond their ability to replenish themselves, groundwater pollution from fertilizers, et cetera, et cetera. Food is cheap because the energy to produce it and ship it the average thirteen hundred miles from the field to the plate has been cheap. And there are the social costs of a nation that no longer has any relationship to the natural world, to the source of its food, and to the agrarian principles that were so much a part of our beginnings as a country.

There are those who are working hard to reinvent the food system so that individual, environmental, and social health do not need to be casualties of eating. Farmers like myself are not only growing food in ways that are safe to eat and considerate to the land, but they are using their farms as platforms for education and social and community health. The focus is shifting away from organic to the greater importance of creating more sustainable *regional* food systems. *Local* is now becoming the catchword (as it should). The financial costs and the costs in human lives and environmental degradation of oil as the primary energy source are becoming clearer to folks.

Many of the folks like myself who grow for their local communities are demanding that they be paid on parity with other professionals. There is an increasing recognition that farming is not just some form of drudgery but that it is an art and a craft and an honorable profession. But folks still have this underlying expectation that food should be cheap. They complain at the farmers' market when well-grown food is being sold at its true cost of production. But when is the last time you heard of someone complaining to their doctor about the prices they charge? If we paid for food up front, if we supported farmers to do their work well and take care of the land we may not need so many doctors (or lawyers or . . .).

Ultimately, the question of unequal access to pure food is far more complex than just the price of food; it really demands that we look deeper at broader economic and social problems. Community gardens, urban agriculture as a significant international movement, access to land and land reform, encouraging young people to consider farming as a profession—all these things can help, but more fundamental structural and societal changes are required if we are to make sure that everyone has access to pure food.

Epilogue

In the introduction to the paperback version of my book *The Middle Mind*, I responded to a question that had been hurled at me by many of my readers. "Fine. Now, *what am I supposed to do?*" At first, my response was like Voltaire's response to the criticism that he had nothing to put in the place of the Christianity he vilified: "What! A ferocious animal has sucked the blood of my family; I tell you to get rid of that beast, and you ask me, what shall we put in its place!" (quoted in Gay, 391). But eventually I came up with a little formula that perhaps at the time was just a way of getting me off the hook but that—after these interviews and the long thinking-through and writing of this book—seems to me pretty much on the mark. I suggested, and suggest still, three things.

Misbehave. Make something beautiful. Try to win.

Is that a politic or an aesthetic? Is it Christian? Is it even spiritual? For me, it is simply the expression of a loyalty to life in a context that in myriad ways tempts us to be disloyal to life. It is as close as I can come to the most beautiful expression in the New Testament, the suggestion that there are "living waters" and that we ought to be part of them. It is the spiritual stream, Walden's "liquid joy." It is the essence of *The Spirit of Disobedience*.

Notes

Introduction

1. Garry Wills, "The Day the Enlightenment Went Out," *New York Times*, November 4, 2004.

2. I will have more to say about Mr. Maher later under the heading of the Holy Whore, but I'd like to take the opportunity to ask, Why is He-who-sleeps-with-bunnies a plausible advocate for the Enlightenment? Actually, now that I've asked that question, it's obvious. Maher is merely one in a long line of libertines who have happily embraced the Enlightenment's critique of Christian morality going back to de Sade, Casanova, and more mythical figures like Don Juan. Libertines rationalize their desires as the virtues of a liberated soul.

3. This is an egregious abbreviation of Kant's complex and remarkable moral system. Those familiar with his thought will simply have to excuse me and move on.

4. This is the heart of Friedrich Nietzsche's criticism of Kant. Kant didn't fool Nietzsche; he was all too Christian ("the Tartuffery of old Kant," he writes). Kant claimed to have discovered a new "faculty," but Nietzsche replied, no, you *invented* a new faculty and, worse than that, in *your own image*. And your own image, it turns out, is finally not so different from the old image of Western man. For all his revolutionary gestures, Kant finally returned "home to the hive."

5. For an extended discussion of this subject, see John Ralston Saul's *Voltaire's Bastards: The Dictatorship of Reason in the West*.

6. Interestingly, the first draft of the Declaration read, "We hold these truths to be sacred and undeniable." In either version, Jefferson reveals a philosophical desperation about how to claim that these "truths" are really true. But claim them he did because politically he *had to*. The metaphysical details could be filled in later.

7. Donald Kaul, "So, Iraq War Was a Good Idea, after All?" *The Pantagraph*, January 1, 2006, C3.

8. In all fairness to the Pharisees, who get very short and rough treatment in the New Testament, they'd seen Jesus's type before. Since Alexander the Great's conquest of Persia, Babylon, and Egypt in the fourth century B.C., and the deep penetration of Greek culture into the Middle East, Jewish culture had been fighting to maintain its own identity. The Old Testament books of Maccabees describe the armed and violent resistance of the orthodox Jewish community to the efforts of the Greek authorities (so-called Seleucians, after Seleucus, one of Alexander's generals) to forbid the practice of their religion in old Judea. The Maccabean revolt strongly emphasized obedience to the laws of observance in the Torah, the first five books of the Old Testament, as a sign of religious, cultural, and political loyalty. Those Jews who were willing to adapt to Hellenistic culture were called "apostates." (The familiar division for us between the modern secular Jew and the Hasidic or orthodox Jew has this deep history.) Jesus would clearly have been seen as an apostate precisely because he failed the oldest test of allegiance: unqualified observance of the Torah. Which should only make it all the clearer why, for the Jews of the time, Jesus was not simply a heretic, he was a political traitor and collaborator. He, like the Jewish philosopher Philo before him, threatened cultural assimilation, racial dilution, and the eventual disappearance of the Jewish nation. Philo's Platonic notion of Logos had a powerful influence on the Gospel of John and the earliest Christian theology. In retrospect, the Pharisees were not wrong to worry that what Christianity promised was a Hellenized Judaism. As Will Durant once put it, "Christianity was the last great creation of the ancient pagan world."

9. I guess that Christian fundamentalists stop reading after the first four "synoptic" books of the Bible. Because otherwise just what the hell kind of literalists are they? It is bewildering.

Chapter 1 Imagination Dead Imagine

1. Or, as President Eisenhower put it during a business dip in the 1950s, "Buy anything" (quoted in Shi, *The Simple Life*, 250).

2. Can't you just imagine the sequel to this thing? A handsome but malevolent CIA scientist (great-grandson to a Nazi scientist who nearly succeeded in cloning the perfect SS storm trooper just months before the end of the war) uses his grandfather's old notes to crack the anointed one's genetic code. So, they're going to clone Him. In time, He'll become the head of the International Monetary Fund and then president of the United

States. This novel will of course make a great feature film combining *The Boys from Brazil*, *The Manchurian Candidate*, and a terrific second-coming thriller about the real anti-Christ, the U.S. president, as if we didn't already know that!

3. Or perhaps it's that the shock of his father's death has turned Hamlet toward the Stoic asceticism of Marcus Aurelius. How like Hamlet he sounds when, in the *Meditations*, he writes, "Observe how ephemeral and worthless human things are, and what was yesterday a little mucus, tomorrow will be a mummy or ashes. . . . The whole space of man's life is but little, and yet with what troubles it is filled . . . and with what a wretched body it must be passed! . . . Turn it inside out, and see what kind of thing it is" (as quoted in Durant, 445).

Chapter 2   Beyond the Golden Rule

1. Conrad echoes Jesus's famous harangue against the Pharisees in Matthew 23:27: "You hypocrites, you are like whitewashed tombs."

2. You know, I'm not even going to bother to develop the fact that the Acts of the Apostles in the New Testament reads at times like a prototype for the *Communist Manifesto*. "The community of believers was of one heart and mind, and no one claimed that any of his possessions was his own, but they had everything in common. . . . There was no needy person among them, for those who owned property or houses would sell them, bring the proceeds of the sale, and put them at the feet of the apostles, and they were distributed to each according to need" (Acts 4:32–35). Just where, I'd like to know, are our fundamentalists on this one? Just where are our biblical literalists? (Unfortunately, they may have their noses back in Leviticus in the Old Testament. Hey, Christians, wrong book!) Jesus's father's house, he tells us, has many mansions, but that doesn't include invitations to come live in one of Pat Robertson's mansions, which are very much private property. But I won't develop this one because the suggestion that Jesus was some sort of proto-Communist always elicits the most amazing frothing at the mouth and gnashing of the teeth by our brethren whose real faith is in the spirit of capitalism. "Show me a sign, Jesus! Show me that old dollar sign!"

3. These vicious people have diminutive nicknames as if they were puppet characters on a PBS kids show. Here's little monster Grovy, and here's little Condi. But they are beasts and brutes, wolves in sheep's clothing.

4. There is nothing in the world more important, according to pop psychology, than "having our needs met." It's the sort of sentiment that is received on television talk shows with groans of sympathy from the audience.

"I left my wife and kids and moved to a new state. Now my wife is a clerk at Wal-Mart, and my daughter spends a lot of time burning herself with cigarettes or cultivating her legs with the garden rake."

"Oh, that's sad. Why did you leave?"

"My needs weren't getting met."

"Well, then, you had to go, didn't you? By the way, what are your needs? I have some needs myself, you know. Maybe we can do some need matching after the show."

This is all only one small step from having your needs met in the community of web-based "dating" clubs, where ever more of us desperately seek the human contact denied us in daily life.

5. It is worth noting, in this regard, author Paul Verhaeghen's recent decision not to accept prize money for winning the Flemish Culture Award for Fiction—the Belgian equivalent of the National Book Award—worth 12,500 euros. Said Verhaeghen, "I have made the calculation. If I would accept the 12,500 euros associated with this award, about $5,000 would flow into the American Treasury. I could pretend that this money will be used to finance public schools or medical care, or will help to alleviate the suffering of the forty million Americans who live below the poverty line. But who would I be kidding? The president just asked Congress for an extra $120 billion in emergency funds for the war. I gladly accept the award, but the money—no, that I cannot accept. This money would be paid for in human blood." Author disclosure: I accepted money for writing this book. I gave some of it to a parrot foundation and some of it to a nonprofit literary press. Other than that, guilty as charged.

6. *New York Times*, January 12, 2004, A23.

7. Isn't it interesting that the word *job* spells the name of the biblical character Job? To me that coincidence lends a whole new level of meaning to Job's complaint, "I despise my life." To which the God of jobs replies, "Gird up your loins." Go to work.

8. *New York Times*, December 23, 2005, A14.

9. "Forced to Work off the Clock, Some Fight Back," *New York Times*, November 19, 2004, A1.

10. And not just the cod. According to a report in the *New York Times*, January 5, 2006, researchers from "Memorial University in St. John's, Newfoundland, found a decline of 89 to 98 percent in just a 17-year span . . . in the populations of five fish species: roundnose grenadier, onion-eye grenadier, blue hake, spiny eel and spinytail skate." They now exist in such low numbers that they are in practical terms extinct.

11. *New York Times*, September 17, 2003, A3.

12. "Big and Blue in the USA," *Orion On-line.*

Chapter 3   Confessions of a Holy Whore

1. All "fair trade" organizations and markets (from which affluent and modestly conscientious Western consumers buy coffee and folk art) are an acknowledgment of this exploitation and this implicit racism. The fact that we don't understand fair trade in this way, but rather as yet another marker of our fundamental benevolence, is only a sign that, as Nietzsche put it, we are "strangers to ourselves."

2. Hillary Johnson and Susan A. Stranahan, "America's Dirty War: The Deadly Cost of Radioactive Tank Busters," *Rolling Stone*, October 2, 2003.

3. Quoted in *In These Times*, February 2006, 47.

4. From Postrel's web site.

Chapter 4   The Spirit of Disobedience

1. Tax deductions for charitable contributions are, by the way, a form of "venial sin," according to the logic of the Roman Catholic catechism, because they pervert the essential human virtue of charity by turning it into self-interest. But that's OK because the wealthy can now structure their charitable giving, through so-called supporting organizations, so that their charitable giving never actually has to give anything to anyone. Charity is just another tax-dodge loophole for the superwealthy. Charity is just another term in the shell game that the wealthy play with—and often with the connivance of—the IRS (Stephanie Strom, "A Tax Benefit That Bypasses Idea of Charity," *New York Times*, April 25, 2005, A1). This form of charity is, in Simone Weil's words, "a good without light" (71). Or, as Thoreau put it, "There is no odor so bad as that which arises from goodness tainted" (55).

2. "Pastor Resigns after Political Spat: Ousted Congregants Say He Mixed Politics and Religion," Associated Press, May 11, 2005.

3. "The Passion of the Christians: The Religious Right Could Well Decide the Coming Election," *The Economist*, October 2, 2004, 34.

4. Even more remarkable, the three most pressing social and political conflicts of our time were the most pressing conflicts of fifth century B.C. Greece. Religious skeptics like Euripides fought against the utterly super-

stitious tradition of the ancient Gods; working people (*demos*) fought revolution after revolution against the landed *oligarchs*; and, of course, the West fought against the East and the Great King of the Persian Empire. This is remarkable, but it also gives a sort of matter-of-fact obviousness to what is on first blush one of Nietzsche's most dubious claims: that every generation of humanity fights the same fight in "the eternal return of the same." We're still fighting over religion, plutocracy, and endlessly, it seems, with the East. The only thing more amazing than this is the fact that we always see these issues as somehow uniquely the burden of our own moment.

5. Witness the Democratic Faith Working Group in the House, and Harry Reid's web site "Word to the Faithful."

6. "Can't a Retail Behemoth Pay More?" *New York Times*, May 4, 2005.

7. Compare Marx in the *Communist Manifesto*: the workman "becomes an appendage of the machine, and it is only the most simple, most monotonous, and most easily acquired knack, that is required of him."

8. Thoreau coined this phrase a full century before Malvina Reynolds saw the "little boxes on the hillside" of Daly City, California. Weirdly, people now pay a fortune for the privilege of living in one of Thoreau's quaint and historic New England "boxes," ditto for Reynolds's stucco cottages in Daly City.

9. Simone Weil: "The enlightened goodwill of men acting in an individual capacity is the only possible principle of social progress" (quoted in Miles, 132). I think Nietzsche, Thoreau, and Weil would make a most interesting trinity for the next revolution.

10. This spiritualized sense of attention to the world can even be traced back to Virgil's *Georgics*, his great poem on the cultivation of the earth: "But meanwhile time flies, flies irreparably, while we, charmed with love [of our theme: agriculture], linger around every single detail" (Durant, 238).

11. "Some Fear Catastrophe from Amazon Highway," Associated Press, May 28, 2005.

12. All quotes are from Jeremy Leggett, *Half Gone: Oil, Gas, Hot Air and the Global Energy Crisis* (London: Portobello Books, 2006). A very similar scenario is predicted by some economists for both the housing market and for industrial agriculture. See Michael Hudson's "The New Road to Serfdom: An Illustrated Guide to the Coming Real Estate Collapse," *Harper's Magazine*, May 2006; and Alan Guebart's syndicated column for the week of April 23, 2006, "Myth Buster Might Be Newest Superhero for Farmers." Guebart notes that it takes ten to fifteen calories of energy for every calorie of food energy produced by industrial agriculture. He concludes, "At $70 per barrel of crude, this 'industrial' food model will soon crack like a robin's egg."

Bibliography

Barthelme, Donald. "Me and Miss Mandible." In *Come Back, Dr. Caligari*. Boston: Little, Brown, 1964.

Brooks, David. *Bobos in Paradise: The New Upper Class and How They Got There*. New York: Simon & Schuster, 2000.

Brown, Dan. *The Da Vinci Code*. New York: Doubleday, 2003.

Conrad, Joseph. "Heart of Darkness." In *Youth*. New York: Collier, 1928.

Durant, Will. *Caesar and Christianity*. New York: Simon & Schuster, 1944.

Emerson, Ralph Waldo. *Essays and Lectures* New York: Library of America, 1983.

———. *The Essential Writings of Ralph Waldo Emerson*. New York: Modern Library Classics, 2000.

Fassbinder, Rainer Werner. *The Anarchy of the Imagination: Interviews, Essays, Notes*. Baltimore: Johns Hopkins University Press, 1992.

Franken, Al. *Lies and the Lying Liars Who Tell Them*. New York: Dutton, 2003.

Galbraith, John Kenneth. *The Affluent Society*. Boston: Houghton Mifflin, 1958.

Gay, Peter. *The Enlightenment: The Rise of Modern Paganism*. New York: Norton, 1965.

Gogol, Nikolai. *Dead Souls*. New York: Barnes & Noble Classics, 2005. (Originally published in 1842.)

Goodman, Paul. *Growing Up Absurd*. New York: Random House, 1960.

Greene, Graham. *The Power and the Glory*. New York: Penguin Classics, 1990.

Heidegger, Martin. *What Is Called Thinking?* New York: Harper & Row, 1968.

Jacoby, Susan. *Freethinkers: A History of American Secularism*. New York: Metropolitan Books, 2004.

Kant, Immanuel. *Foundations of the Metaphysics of Morals*. Trans. Lewis White Beck. Indianapolis: Bobbs-Merrill, 1969. (Originally published in 1785.)

————. *Critique of Practical Reason.* Trans. and ed. Lewis White Black. New York: Macmillan, 1993. (Originally published in 1788.)

Katz, Robert. *Love Is Colder Than Death.* New York: Random House, 1987.

Kirkland, Edward C. *A History of American Economic Life.* New York: Appleton, Century, Crofts, 1932.

Maher, Bill. *When You Ride Alone, You Ride with Bin Laden.* New York: New Millennium, 2003.

Marx, Karl. *Capital.* New York: Modern Library, 1906.

Matthiessen, F. O. *American Renaissance.* London: Oxford University Press, 1941.

Miles, Sian. *Simone Weil: An Anthology.* New York: Grove, 1986.

Morgan, George Allen. *What Nietzsche Means.* New York: Harper Torchbooks, 1975.

Nietzsche, Friedrich. *The Philosophy of Nietzsche.* New York: Modern Library, 1927.

Paine, Thomas. *The Age of Reason.* Paris: Barrois, 1794.

Paley, William. *Principles of Moral and Political Philosophy.* Philadelphia: Dobson, 1785.

Postrel, Virginia. *The Future and Its Enemies: The Growing Conflict over Creativity, Enterprise, and Progress.* New York: Free Press, 1998.

————. *The Substance of Style: How the Rise of Aesthetic Value Is Remaking Commerce, Culture, and Consciousness.* New York: HarperCollins, 2003.

Proust, Marcel. *In Search of Lost Time.* New York: Modern Library, 2003. (Originally published in 1927.)

Reich, Robert. *Reason: Why Liberals Will Win the Battle for America.* New York: Knopf, 2004.

Ricoeur, Paul. *The Conflict of Interpretations.* Evanston, IL: Northwestern University Press, 1974.

————. *Figuring the Sacred.* Minneapolis: Fortress, 1995.

Rogers, Heather. *Gone Tomorrow: The Hidden Life of Garbage.* New York: New Press, 2005.

Rousseau, Jean-Jacques. *The Social Contract, or Principles of Political Right.* Cambridge: Cambridge University Press, 1997.

Ruskin, John. *Munera Pulveris.* In *The Works of John Ruskin.* New York: Wiley, 1885.

————. *Unto This Last.* In *The Works of John Ruskin.* New York: Wiley, 1885.

Saul, John Ralston. *Voltaire's Bastards: The Dictatorship of Reason in the West.*

New York: Vintage Books, 1993.

Shakespeare, William. *Hamlet*. New York: Penguin Classics, 1981.

Shi, David E. *The Simple Life: Plain Living and High Thinking in American Culture*. New York: Oxford University Press, 1985.

Thoreau, Henry David. *Walden*. New York: Signet Classics, 1960.

Weber, Max. *The Protestant Ethic and the Spirit of Capitalism*. London: Penguin Books, 2002.

Weil, Simone. *Gravity and Grace*. London: Routledge, 2002.

Žižek, Slavoj. *The Puppet and the Dwarf: The Perverse Core of Christianity*. Cambridge, MA: MIT Press, 2003.

Acknowledgments

First, to the humans involved in the conceiving and writing of this book. I wish to thank Gideon Weil, with whom this idiosyncratic project was first begun. I owe him my deepest thanks. Also, to Roger Hodge of *Harper's Magazine* for his extraordinary support and encouragement over the last five years. To my agent, Emma Parry, for her unreasonable persistence, confidence, and utter good faith. To Ewa Chrusciel for being the good shepherd during a season of spiritual fear and trembling. As ever, to my wife, Georganne Rundblad, who stood consistently at my back in order to whack my shoulders when I fell from meditation into mere sleep. Lastly, to my editor Peter Richardson, who for some reason found in my cranky complaints about my last publisher a reason to become my new publisher. Unaccountable behavior but most welcome. I'm grateful to him.

Bookish debts. First and foremost, to the work of Paul Ricoeur. I cite Ricoeur on several occasions in this book, but that doesn't begin to account for my obligation to his work. This book should be read as if through a limpid blue wash of Ricoeur's humane, varied, and *thoughtful* work. He above all allowed me to see how thinking itself is spirit. I should also acknowledge the work of Slavoj Žižek whose book *The Puppet and the Dwarf: The Perverse Core of Christianity* was an inspiration to me and a constant touchstone

173

for this work. The phrase "Culture of Total Work" in my subtitle is from Josef Pieper's book *Leisure: The Basis of Culture*. It is an apt descriptor of my material on jobs and work, but it is borrowed. Finally, portions of this work first appeared in *Stop Smiling*, *The Village Voice*, and *Harper's Magazine*.

Index

Ableman, Michael, 150–159
Abortion, 103, 111
Abundance, 50, 51
Africa, colonialism in, 49
The Age of Reason (Paine), 6
Agriculture, 150–159
  and deforestation in Brazil, 66–67, 116
  energy resources required for, 168n12
  in Europe, 142
  organic, 91–93, 150–159
  of Quaker community in Costa Rica, 115–116
Ali: Fear Eats the Soul, 71–72
Alienation, 3, 28, 106, 126
  and isolation, 52–57
Allende, Salvador, 63
Alliant Techsystems, 82
Amazon forest, 22, 66–67, 116
America
  concept of, 86, 121
  and national interests, 20, 64
  statement of love for, 85–87
Aronowitz, Stanley, 59
Art, 21, 35–36, 75
  farming as, 156–157
  in public education, 43
  and social function of imagination, 33
  spiritual content of, 39, 42–43
Arts and crafts movement, 16

Association for the Study of Peak Oil, 117
Attention to present moment, 110, 114
Augustine, Saint, 133
Authority, 73, 82
  legitimacy of, 145–147
  and obedience in public education, 9–10
  in Republican Party, 146
Automobiles, 134, 141–145
  and highway system, 57, 58–59, 143
  and oil dependence, 118, 141
  walking as alternative to, 58–59
Awareness, sense of, 114

Baader, Andreas, 73
Bankruptcy
  personal financial, 51, 136
  spiritual, 81
Barthelme, Donald, 10
Barton, Anne, 38
Barzun, Jacques, 99
Baxter, Richard, 51
Beckett, Samuel, 19, 135
Being, 18
Bennett, William, 121
Bentley, Roger, 117
Berry, Wendell, 149
Betrayal, 39, 106
Beware of a Holy Whore, 74
Bhagavad Gita, 54

Bible, 6
  Acts, 165n2
  consulted by jury, 95–96
  Corinthians, 15, 106
  Luke, 51
  Matthew, 11
  Philippians, 12
  Psalms, 62
  Revelations, 30
  Romans, 14, 15
Blake, William, 45, 104
Bloom, Harold, 38
Bobos in Paradise (Brooks), 93
Booth, Roger, 117
Brazil, deforestation in, 66–67, 116
Brokeback Mountain, 39–42
Brooks, David, 93, 94
Brooks, Van Wyck, 99, 135
Brower, David, 126
Brown, Dan, *The Da Vinci Code* novel,
  21, 31–34, 35, 42
Brustein, Robert, 135
Burns, Ken, 121
Bush, George W., 48, 76, 81, 101, 106, 147
  election of 2004, 1–2, 100, 122–123
Bush, Jeb, 58

Campbell, Colin, 117
Capital (Marx), 3, 5
Capitalism, 16, 61, 69, 96, 97–98, 101–102
  and common abundance, 51
  corporate, 22, 29, 66, 70, 72, 88, 101, 124
  and fascism, 70–71, 72
  global, 118
  individualism of, 18
  Marx on, 2–5, 11, 12–13
  and oil resources, 117–118
  power accumulation in, 88
  profit in, 97, 98, 132
  Ricoeur on, 30
  and terrorism, 85
  time at work in, 132–133
Catholic Church, 31–34, 99
Central Intelligence Agency, 63, 64, 82
Charitable gifts, 69, 98, 167n1
Cheney, Dick, 48, 62, 82, 100, 106

Chicago, IL, 143
China, traditional agriculture in,
  150–151
Chomsky, Noam, 83, 84–85
Christianity, 5–6, 14–18, 39
  in *The Da Vinci Code,* 21, 31–34, 35, 42
  and Enlightenment division, 95–104
  morality of equivalence in, 50–51
  and Republican Party, 98, 100
Clark, Wesley, 85
Cold War era, 61
Collateral damage, 67
Colonialism, 49
Common sense, 8, 9, 135
Communalism, 18
  agrarian-based, Ableman in, 152–154
Complicity, 56, 57, 63, 75
Conrad, Joseph, 49
Conservatives, love for America
  statements of, 85–86
Consumer confidence, 23
Consumption and consumer
  confidence, 23
Copper resources, 117
Corporate capitalism, 22, 29, 66, 70, 72,
  88, 101, 124
Cost/benefit analysis, 55, 64
Costa Rica, community of American
  Quakers in, 115–116
Coulter, Ann, 78, 83–84, 88
Counter-Enlightenment, 104, 105, 111
Counterculture of 1960s, 83, 118
Couric, Katie, 53
Cowboy stoicism, 40, 41
Creativity, 18, 126
  opportunities for, 60–62, 89, 91, 130
  in research of teachers, 59–60, 89
Credit card interest rates, 51
Critique of Practical Reason (Kant), 5
Cruelty, 63–64
Cuba, 84, 127
Cultural capital, 61
Culture of death, 12, 102, 111, 114, 118
Culture of life, 18
Culture Theater, 78
Culture war, 78, 102, 121, 123

Cunningham, Randy, 88

Da Silva, Luiz Inácio Lula, 66–67
The Da Vinci Code (Brown), 21, 31–34, 35, 42
Daddy Party, 146–147
De Graaf, John, 124–134, 156
De Tocqueville, Alexis, 122, 123
Dead Souls (Gogol), 65
Dean, Howard, 76, 113
The Decameron (Boccaccio), 54
Declaration of Independence, 8, 163n6
Deforestation in Brazil, 66–67, 116
DeLay, Tom, 88, 105
Democracy, 87, 112, 123
Democratic Party, 2, 84–85, 98, 100, 146
Detroit, illiteracy rate in, 84–85
Devoto, Bernard, 136
Dialectical materialism, 13
Distractions, and attention to present moment, 114
Divorce, 53
Dobbs, Lou, 25
Dole, organic foods of, 92 93
Drifting in life, 110–111
Duany, Andres, 137
Duty, 48, 100, 105, 112

Earth Day, 128, 129
Economic rationalism, 60, 101, 102, 104
Education, 59–62
    art appreciation in, 43
    curriculum decisions in, 3–4
    goals in, 56
    and illiteracy rate, 84–85
    obedience to authority in, 9–10
    as workforce preparation, 4, 131
Edwards, Jonathan, 104
Eisenhower, Dwight D., 164n1
Election of 2004, 1–2, 100, 122–123
Emerson, Ralph Waldo, 19, 29, 104, 105, 112
Enlightenment, 2, 5–9
    and Christianity division, 95–104
    and counter-Enlightenment, 104, 105, 111

Environmental changes, 22, 48, 66–67, 116, 136
    from agriculture, 158
    and love for America, 86
Epicurus, 18
Equivalence, 50–51
Erasmus, 99
Ethereal realm, 110
Evangelicals, 1–2, 50, 99, 100
Evans, Christopher, 2
Evil, 48–50, 69–70
    and duty, 48, 112
    institutionalized, 48, 62, 88
    radical, 48, 49–50, 69
    self-interest and self-defeat in, 62–63
Exchange value compared to use value, 114
The Experience of Place (Hiss), 137
Exploitation, 4, 12, 71, 102, 111, 113, 167n1
Exxon-Mobil, 148

Fahrenheit 9/11, 99
Fair trade organizations, 167n1
Faith, 30–31
Falwell, Jerry, 105
Farming. *See* Agriculture
Fascism, 70–71, 72, 82
Fassbinder, Rainer Werner, 70–75, 78, 85, 87–88
Feeling, 104
Ferry, Jules, 6–7
Fields of Plenty: A Farmer's Journey in Search of Real Food and the People Who Grow It (Ableman), 151, 152, 156
Figuring the Sacred (Ricoeur), 50
Fish population, decline in, 66, 166n10
Flag burning, 80–81
Florida, health insurance for low-income children in, 57–58
Food, 150–159
    as fundamental, 113, 114, 150–159
    organic, 91–93, 150–159
Foreign policy, 48
    cruelty and violence in, 63–64

and isolation from others, 54–55
and national interests, 64
and profits from war, 82
Foucault, Michel, 21
Foundations of the Metaphysics of Morals (Kant), 5
France, 99, 140
Frank, Thomas, 88
Franken, Al, 76, 84–86, 87, 88
Franklin, Benjamin, 9
Fraser, Donald M., 91
Free market, 30, 87, 93, 94, 98, 113
Freedom, 67, 80–81, 102, 103
Freethinkers: A History of American Secularism (Jacoby), 99
Fromm, Erich, 126
Fukuyama, Francis, 93
Fundamentals, 30, 113–114, 121–159
food, 150–159
home, 113, 114, 134–150
time, 124–134
The Future and Its Enemies (Postrel), 94

Galbraith, John Kenneth, 51, 96
Gandhi, Mahatma, 52
The Geography of Nowhere (Kunstler), 138
Gibson, Mel, 99
Ginsberg, Allen, 105
Gnosticism, 32
God, 5–6, 50
Goddess of Reason, 6
Gogol, Nikolai, 65
Goldberg, Bernie, 84
Golden Rule, 11, 17, 46–47, 61, 69, 88, 90
failure of, 63
self-interest in, 16
Gone Tomorrow: The Hidden Life of Garbage (Rogers), 93
Good, 17, 21, 108
greater good, 47
public good, 50
Goodman, Paul, 25, 89–90
Grace, balance with gravity, 116
Grasso, Richard, 69
Gravity, balance with grace, 116

Greater good, 47
Greene, Graham, 13
Greenhouse, Steven, 66
Gross,, Terry, 77
Gulf Wars, 49

Halliburton, 82
Hamilton, David, 135
Hamlet (Shakespeare), 35–39, 42, 45–47, 70, 105, 165n3
Hannity, Sean, 78
Havemeyer, H. O., 96
Health insurance, 57–58
Herbert, Bob, 57–58
Heart of Darkness (Conrad), 49
Hegel, Georg Wilhelm Friedrich, 18, 105
Heidegger, Martin, 79
Herbert, Bob, 57–58
Highway system, 57, 58–59, 143
Hiss, Tony, 137
Hitchens, Christopher, 78
Hitler, Adolf, 48
Holy Fool, 71–72
Holy Grail, 31
Holy Whore, 70, 74, 75, 87–88
Home
as fundamental, 113, 114, 134–150
isolation in, 54, 149
in suburban developments, 109, 136, 138–142, 149
Hope, 124
Horace, 33
Hurricane Katrina, 97
Hussein, Saddam, 48
Hypocrisy, 46, 47–52, 63

Illich, Ivan, 127
Illiteracy in Detroit, 84–85
Imagination, 33, 35, 104, 105, 111, 113, 131
In Search of Lost Time (Proust), 63
Instinct, 104
Intelligence
in Democratic and Republican states, 2
resentment of, 145
Intelligent design, 8, 95

Interest rates on credit cards, 51
Intuition, 104
Iraq, 54, 82, 106
Isolation, 52–57, 89
  in home, 54, 149
Ivins, Molly, 76

Jackson, Andrew, 122
Jacobs, Jane, 137
Jacoby, Susan, 99
Jesus, 11, 14, 15, 39, 51, 90, 97, 104, 164n8
  and Mary Magdalene, 31, 33, 34
Jewish law and culture, 14, 15, 164n8
Job (biblical), 166n7
Jobs and work. *See* Work
John Paul II, Pope, 12, 102
Johnson, Kirk, 95, 96
Judge, Mike, 24, 25, 26, 28
Justice, 17–18, 49, 50, 88

Kagemusha (film), 40
Kant, Immanuel, 1, 5–8, 11, 14, 71, 97,
    163n3, 163n4
  on evil, 48, 69
  on moral maxim, 46
Kaplan, James, 60
Kaul, Donald, 8
Kerry, John, 113
Kindness, natural disposition to, 63
King, Larry, 53, 79
Kingdom of Ends, 11
Klett, Renate, 72
Koresh, David, 30
Krier, Leon, 138
Kunstler, James Howard, 68, 117,
    134–150, 156
Kurosawa, Akira, 40

Labor
  exploitation of, 71, 102
  Marx on, 3–5
  nature of, in *Office Space* movie,
    24–29
Lee, Ang, 39, 40, 41, 42
Legality, 107, 112, 116
Legitimacy of authority, 145–147

Levittown West, 138
Lewis, Huey, 86
Liberalism, 1, 2, 85–86
Lies and the Lying Liars Who Tell Them
    (Franken), 84
Life insurance policies on Wal-Mart
    employees, 65–66
Limbaugh, Rush, 78
Local and regional food systems, 159
Love, 18, 115
  for America, statements of, 85–87
  commandment of Jesus on, 90
  for neighbor, 46, 88, 103
  unfulfilled, 40
Love is Colder Than Death, 71
Loyalty to life, 115

Machiavelli, 37
Magdalene, Mary, 31, 33, 34
Maggi, Blairo, 67
Maher, Bill, 2, 78–79, 80–81, 83, 85, 87,
    163n2
Marcuse, Herbert, 126
Market freedom, 67
The Marriage of Maria Braun (film),
    70–71
Marx, Karl, 1, 14, 66, 107
  on alienation, 3, 126
  on capitalism, 2–5, 11, 12–13
  compared to Thoreau, 107, 108, 109,
    110, 114
  on value of time, 127
Marxism, 5, 12–13
Mass consciousness, 121–122, 139
Materialism, 126, 127, 128
Mather, Cotton, 104
Maurois, Andre, 6
McDonald's, 23, 84
McGuane, Tom, 135
Means of production, 3, 66
Mencken, H. L., 135
Mercantile economy, 16
The Merchant of Four Seasons, 73
*The Middle Mind: Why Americans Don't
    Think for Themselves* (White),
    76–78, 131, 161

Mill, John Stuart, 16
Mommy Party, 146
Money
  flow of, 59
  sociality of, 56, 57
  time exchanged for, 108–109, 133
Moore, Michael, 76, 77, 99, 121
Morality, 9, 10, 46, 47
Morris, William, 16
Mosaic law, 14
Mumford, Lewis, 137
Municipal planning, 144–145

Nader, Ralph, 128, 131
National identity, 20, 121–124
  capitalism in, 96
  and gesture of self-alienation, 106
  and mass consciousness, 121–122
  role of Christianity and
    Enlightenment in, 95–101
  and united we stand, 86
National interests, 20, 64
Nature, 18
Nazi Germany, 48
Needs, meeting of, 53, 165–166n4
Negri, Antonio, 56
New Fundamentalism, 123–124
New Orleans, impact of Hurricane
  Katrina in, 97
New Urbanist movement, 144
New York City, 143–144
Newtithing Group, 69
Nietzsche, Friedrich, 10, 19, 41, 52, 75,
  90, 95, 109–110, 111, 163n4
Nixon, Richard, 128
Nonequivalence, 51
Novels as instruments of social
  change, 136, 137

Obedience in public education, 9–10
Office Space (film), 21, 24–29, 30
Oil resources, 48, 63, 117–118, 138, 139,
  140–141, 148
Olson, Charles, 105
O'Reilly, Bill, 78

Organic foods and farming, 91–93,
  150–159
Organic Valley farmer co-op, 91–93
Organized crime, government as, 82
Orwell, George, 20
Outside, notion of, 70, 72–73, 115, 125
Overspecialization, 137

Paine, Thomas, 6, 9, 123
Palast, Greg, 87
Paley, William, 5
Paris Commune, 6
Party of Business, 85, 101
Pascal, Blaise, 50
The Passion of the Christ (film), 99
Patriotism, 85–87, 112
Paul, Saint, 12, 14, 15, 50, 106, 119
Peak Oil, 117, 148
Pinter, Harold, 20
Pope, Alexander, 16
Postrel, Virginia, 93–94
Pound, Ezra, 105
Poverty in time, 128, 129, 133
Power accumulation in capitalism, 88
The Power and the Glory (Greene), 13
Predator missile, 101
Prejudice, 7
Priests, sexual abuse of children by, 79
Principles of Moral and Political
  Philosophy (Paley), 5
Prison systems, 55, 106
Productivity
  exchanged for time, 127, 128
  in research of professors, 60
Profit, 76, 97, 98, 132
  in motivation of workers, 26–27
  in organic farming, 92, 93
  self-interest in, 67
  in war, 49, 82
Property rights, 18, 97, 103
Proust, Marcel, 63, 64
Public good, 50

Quaker community in Costa Rica,
  115–116

Quality of life, 132

Racism, 53
Radical evil, 48, 49–50, 69
Radioactive materials in tank-buster
    shells, 82
Ratio, 104
Rationalism, economic, 60, 101, 102, 104
Rawls, John, 11
Reagan, Ronald, 97
Reason, 1, 6–9, 17, 39, 104, 105
*Reason: Why Liberals Will Win the Battle
    for America* (Reich), 17, 99
Reformation era, 99
Refusal strategy, 18, 106, 113, 118, 124, 125
    organic foods in, 91, 92
    socialized, 89
    in spirit of disobedience, 115
Regional food systems, 159
Reich, Robert, 17, 99, 100
Religion, 4, 39
Representative Men (Emerson), 112
Republican Party, 1–2, 84–85, 98, 99,
    100, 146–147
Research of professors, creativity and
    productivity in, 59–60, 89, 130
Revolutionaries, 71, 73–75, 76
    anonymity and futility of, 109
    in czarist Russia, 12–13
    Jesus as, 14, 15
Ricoeur, Paul, 30, 50
Rogers, Heather, 93
Rousseau, Jean-Jacques, 3, 104
Ruskin, John, 11, 16–17, 18, 47–48, 98,
    101, 113
Russian revolution, 12–13

Sabbatical system proposal, 91
Sacred, 34–35, 56
    in *Hamlet*, 35–39
    and secular, 101–102
    time for, 133
San Francisco, CA, 83, 138
Santayana, George, 112
Schygulla, Hanna, 73

Secularists in Democratic Party, 98
Self-defeat, 62–68, 75
Self-evidence, 8
Self-interest, 11, 16, 62–68, 70
Semple, Robert B., Jr., 148
Servility, 14, 57–62
Shakespeare, William, *Hamlet* of,
    35–39, 42, 45–47, 70, 105, 165n3
Shock and awe, 116
Simplicity, 110, 128
Slavery, 3, 18, 105
    part time, 65
Smith, Adam, 16, 96
The Social Contract (Rousseau), 3
Social Darwinians, 100
Social reform movements, 42
Sociality of money, 56, 57
Socialized strategy of refusal, 89
Solitude, 109–110, 126
Species being, 4
Spencer, Herbert, 100
Spiritual bankruptcy, 81
Spirituality
    in art, 39, 42–43
    postinstitutional, 38
Spontaneity, 104
Statistical analysis, 137
Stendahl, 75
Stockholders, returns on investments
    to, 98
The Substance of Style (Postrel), 93
Suburban developments, 109, 118, 136,
    138–142, 149
Surplus value, 2–3
Sustainability, 111, 118, 128

Take Back Your Time Day, 124, 128–129
Taxes, 57–58, 62, 97, 167n1
Teachers, 59–61
    creativity and productivity in
        research activities, 59–60, 89, 130
Ten Commandments, 14–15
Terrorism, 22, 85, 87, 122
Third estate, 99
The Third Man (Welles), 55

Thoreau, Henry David, 3, 9, 18, 19, 20, 21–22, 30–31, 105–114
Time
  as cost of work, 108–109
  exchanged for money, 108–109, 133
  as fundamental, 124–134
Time poverty, 128, 129, 133
Time to Care coalition, 129
Tolerance, 40
Tools for Conviviality (Illich), 127
Torture as routine, 62
Truth, 35

Ugliness, 71, 138, 139–140
United we stand, 86
Urban areas, 137
  automobiles in, 141, 143–144
  farming in, 152, 154–155
Use value compared to exchange value, 114
Utopia, 119, 127

Value
  in fundamentals, 113–114
  surplus value, 2–3
  use value compared to exchange value, 114
Van Ronk, Dave, 23
Verhaeghen, Paul, 166n5
Video games, violent, 102–103
Vietnam War, 127
Voltaire, 6, 99, 104, 161

Wages
  and unpaid work hours, 66
  in Wal-Mart, 64–65, 102
Wal-Mart, 22, 23, 64–66, 91, 101, 102, 117, 123, 131
Walden (Thoreau), 9, 19, 107–108
Walking, 58–59, 133, 142–145
War
  and isolation, 54–55
  profits in, 49, 82
  self-interests in, 49
  against terror, 85, 87

  in Vietnam, 127
Wealth, accumulation of, 16, 50, 69
Wealth of Nations (Smith), 96
Weapons, 82, 90–91, 101
Weber, Max, 60
Weil, Simone, 112, 116
Welles, Orson, 55
Wesley, John, 123
Whalin, George, 102
What is Called Thinking? (Heidegger), 79
When You Ride Alone, You Ride with Bin Laden (Maher), 80
Whitman, Walt, 21, 105
Wild Oats Markets, 92, 157
Wills, Garry, 1–2
Wiretapping, 117
Work
  exploitation in, 71, 102
  in farming, 153–157
  in globalization, 55
  Marx on, 107, 108
  in Office Space movie, 24–29
  sabbatical system proposed, 91
  social relationships in, 56
  of teachers, 59–61
  Thoreau on, 107, 108–109, 110
  time in, 108–109, 124–134
  unpaid, 66
  in useful and good job, 89–90
  virtue of, 108, 110
  in Wal-Mart, 64–66
Work ethic, 132
Workers
  anonymity and futility of, 109
  exploitation of, 71, 102
  Marx on, 3–5
  in Office Space movie, 24–29
  profit motive of, 26–27
  in Wal-Mart, 64–66, 102
World Trade Center terrorist attack, 22

Young, Neil, 155

Žižek, Slavoj, 39, 90, 115

About the Author

Dubbed "a splendidly cranky academic" by Molly Ivins, novelist and social critic CURTIS WHITE is a professor of English at Illinois State University. His previous book, *The Middle Mind: Why Americans Don't Think for Themselves*, was widely acclaimed. His other books include *Monstrous Possibility, Requiem, Memories of My Father Watching TV*, and *The Idea of Home*. His essays have appeared in many publications, including *Harper's Magazine* and *The Village Voice*. He lives in Normal, Illinois, with his wife Georganne Rundblad and their five psittacine companions.

Other Books from PoliPointPress

William Rivers Pitt, *House of Ill Repute: Reflections on War, Lies, and America's Ravaged Reputation.*
Skewers the Bush Administration for its reckless invasions, warrantless wiretaps, lethally incompetent response to Hurricane Katrina and other failures. ISBN: 0-9778253-2-9, $14.95, soft cover.

Jeff Cohen, *Cable News Confidential: My Misadventures in Corporate Media*
Offers a fast-paced romp through the three major cable news channels—Fox CNN, and MSNBC—and delivers a serious message about their failure to cover the most urgent issues of the day. ISBN: 0-9760621-6-X, $14.95, soft cover.

Nomi Prins, *Jacked: How "Conservatives" Are Picking Your Pocket—Whether You Voted For Them or Not.*
Presents Republican policies, scandals and blunders as they relate to the everyday contents of your wallet. ISBN: 0-9760621-8-6, $12.00, soft cover

Yvonne Latty, *In Conflict: Iraq War Veterans Speak Out on Duty, Loss, and the Fight to Stay Alive.*
Features the unheard voices, extraordinary experiences, and personal photographs of a broad mix of Iraq War veterans. ISBN: 0-9760621-4-3 $24.00, hard cover.

Steven Hill, *10 Steps to Repair American Democracy.*
Identifies key problems with American democracy and proposes ten specific reforms to reinvigorate it. ISBN: 0-9760621-5-1 $11.00, soft cover.
The Blue Pages: A Directory of Companies Rated by Their Politics and Practices.
Helps consumers match buying decisions with their political, social and environmental values.
ISBN: 0-9760621-1-9 $9.95, soft cover.

Joe Conason, *The Raw Deal: How the Bush Republicans Plan to Destroy Social Security and the Legacy of the New Deal.*
Describes the well-financed and determined effort to undo the Social Security Act and New Deal programs. ISBN: 0-9760621-2-7 $11.00, soft cover.

John Sperling et al., *The Great Divide: Retro vs. Metro America.*
Explores differences between the so-called "red" and "blue" states and why our nation is so bitterly divided into what the authors call Retro and Metro America. ISBN: 0-09760621-0-0 $19.95, soft cover.
For more information, please visit www.p3books.com.